Henry Vaughan

The Golden Age
of Spiritual Writing

Series editor: David Scott

Lancelot Andrewes: The Private Prayers
Selected and translated by David Scott

George Herbert: Verse and Prose
Selected and introduced by Wendy Cope

Thomas Traherne: Poetry and Prose
Selected and introduced by Denise Inge

Henry Vaughan: Selected Poems
Selected and introduced by Anne Cluysenaar

The Golden Age
of Spiritual Writing

Henry Vaughan
Selected Poems

Selected and introduced by
Anne Cluysenaar

Published in Great Britain in 2004
Society for Promoting Christian Knowledge
Holy Trinity Church
Marylebone Road
London NW1 4DU

British Library Cataloguing-in-Publication Data

A catalogue record for this book is available from the British Library

ISBN 0-281-05542-4

10 9 8 7 6 5 4 3 2 1

Typeset by Wilmaset Ltd, Birkenhead
Printed in Great Britain by Antony Rowe Ltd, Chippenham, Wiltshire

Contents

Acknowledgements

Earlier versions of certain ideas developed here appeared in *Scintilla*, the yearly journal of the Usk Valley Vaughan Association (first issue 1997), and in my introduction to a selection of Henry Vaughan's poems included in *Poets on Poets* (Carcanet in association with Waterstone's, 1997).

I wish to thank the Revd James Coutts, Dr Peter Thomas and Esther de Waal, who read a draft of the introduction and made many useful suggestions. Any remaining errors or infelicities are my own.

The Golden Age of Spiritual Writing

The Golden Age of Spiritual Writing brings together a series of books of English 'spiritual' poetry and prose, selected and introduced by well-known contemporary authors and scholars. Many of the writers on whom this series focuses flourished during the seventeenth century. You may well ask, 'Why concentrate on writers of the seventeenth century? Wasn't it a long time ago?' Historically, that period might well seem 'a long time ago', especially when we consider the huge changes in communications and in scientific understanding, and, yet, looked at with the long view of human history, the seventeenth century is quite recent. It was, in many ways, the beginning of the modern age. We share with the people of that time the struggles and strains of being human, the joys as well as the challenges of the natural world, and the seemingly incontrovertible facts of birth and death. In our religious lives, too, we want to talk about the challenges of new cultures bearing down on what we consider eternal truths, and the relationship between different Christian traditions.

But we do bother about the seventeenth-century writers, and have done with increasing enthusiasm since the early part of the twentieth century, with the name and influence of T. S. Eliot ranking large. I think we bother about them for three main reasons. First, they write well. Second, they tell eternal truths. And third, for our spiritually bewildered age, they fill a dry well with clear, fresh water.

There is something about the English language of this period that has an element of the miraculous. We find this most commonly in the plays of Shakespeare and in the Authorized Version of the Bible: the two books without which any stay on a desert island is deficient. Their language is not so removed from our own that we are utterly confused by it, but it is freshly coined enough to retain its life, its bite and chew. It has the power to evoke in us, physically, the moods, emotions and thoughts the words are trying to express. The words and the rhythms can make us cry and laugh and ponder with a huge intensity. Someone could probably explain this miracle and find it, for sure, in other writers of different ages; but all I want to do is to encourage readers to see if it is true for them about the seventeenth century. However, when it comes to dealing with the translated material of Lancelot Andrewes then different linguistic criteria have to be applied.

The words have to be about something. It is not just a matter of style or sound. The words have to tell us something that we find valuable. This series concentrates on spiritual writers. Each of them refers easily and unashamedly to God, and not infrequently to Jesus Christ as the revelation of God's love in and for the world. They write of sin and prayer, of salvation and love, of death and heaven and hell, and they mean real things by them. The writers precede the growth of rationalism that developed in the eighteenth century. Are we not too grown up and too clever for such things? Are we not, as Eliot put it, banging an antique drum? Each of the books in this series will be at pains to persuade us that this is not so, and more importantly, the writers themselves will do so, too. They take the great spiritual themes of all times and places: desire, fear, decision-making, a sense of wonder and of awe, anxiety and loss, and, by their own vision and breadth of experience, make them reach down to us in our own day.

Reading the great classics of spiritual literature of whatever age today will always be a new thing, it is a new generation that is reading them. Reading Traherne in an era of massive pollution will put his sense of wonder and affection for the natural world in a new political context. Donne's honesty about sex and religion will raise questions about the nature of humanity, which, after Freud, will seem as real as ever. Herbert's gentle, pragmatic ethics might encourage a new generation to reflect on standards of behaviour and the place of an ordered life in a free-floating world. Each of the writers presented in this series will have something to contribute to the contemporary debate. Pondering these questions will be to the benefit of both writer and reader. The echoes of great literature come not only from within the text itself, but also from outside the text. In reading the poetry, the thoughts, the prayers, we make them live again. For people searching for the words that express what they want to say, here in this series will be some familiar resources and, I trust, some revelations.

As editor of the series, I would like to thank all the authors who agreed to contribute. I am especially grateful for the high quality of their work, which has made my task so much easier. I have worked closely throughout with the editorial team at SPCK, especially with Liz Marsh. I am immensely grateful to them for their friendly support and for their decision to take on the publication of this fascinating area of spiritual writing. Without them this series would never have come together.

David Scott
Winchester

Introduction

The Life

Happy those early dayes! when I
Shin'd in my Angell-infancy.
'The Retreate'[1]

Henry Vaughan and his brother Thomas were born in 1621 on Newton Farm in the valley of the river Usk near Brecon. This is an area where smooth bare mountains hang like suspended waves over fertile green pastures. In Henry's own words, 'Wales gave me birth, in the place where Father Usk launches down from the windswept mountains to wander in broad valleys.'[2] Newton Farm had been his mother Denise Morgan's home before her marriage, while Henry's father Thomas Vaughan is thought to have been a younger son of the Vaughans of Tretower Court, the fine fourteenth-century building which still stands just a few miles down the valley.

Evidence suggests that the boys were identical twins,[3] Henry being the first-born and therefore inheritor of Newton Farm. Their brother William was some seven years younger, so the twins must have spent time on their own together, exploring the river, its tributary rills and springs, and the mountains from which they rise. Henry's poetry and Thomas's alchemical writing (sprinkled with poems) carry many hints that, for both of them, these early experiences proved formative. In particular, the twins developed a fascination with water and light. Thomas points to the way his childhood fascination with light intertwined with water became the source of childhood experiments and later of alchemical researches:

> . . . that which took me up much and soon, was the continual action of fire upon water. This Speculation (I know not how) surpris'd my first youth, long before I saw the University and certainly Nature, whose pupil I was, had even then awaken'd many Notions in me, which I met with afterwards, in the Platonick Philosophie. I will not forebear to write, how I had then fansied a certain practice upon water, out of which, even in those childish days, I expected wonders . . .[4]

In the poem 'Midnight', Henry evokes spiritual transformation by means of a comparable image:

> Thy heav'ns (some say,)
> Are a firie-liquid light,
>   Which mingling aye
> Streames, and flames thus to the sight.
>   Come then, my god!
>   Shine on this bloud,
>   And water in one beame,
>   And thou shalt see
>   Kindled by thee
> Both liquors burne, and streame.

*

> . . . *now the Shepheards Star*
> *With beauteous looks smiles on us, though from far.*
> 'Daphnis. An Elegiac *Eclogue*'

By the time they were 11 years old, Henry and Thomas were boarding in the nearby village of Llangattock under the care of the well-known clergyman-tutor, Matthew Herbert. For Henry in particular this proved a most fortunate circumstance. Matthew Herbert loved the Welsh bards as well as the Latin poets and seems to have taken his pupils out onto the river banks at dusk to read their poems amid the distant calling of sheep on the mountain slopes. 'Daphnis. An Elegiac *Eclogue*', which appeared in *Thalia Rediviva*, is thought to evoke the life of Henry and Thomas while under the care of Matthew Herbert, who is perhaps represented there as 'old Amphion'. This early introduction to the ancient bardic tradition of Wales, with its unique insistence on the communal role of the poet, was to become vitally important to Henry. A letter he sent his cousin Aubrey in old age, concerning the bards, is relevant here and may echo a tale told him by his loved tutor.[5] Feeling this letter to be significant for Henry's view of his own task, I have included it in this anthology, and made it the centrepiece of my poem-sequence 'Vaughan Variations'.[6] We might also say that the twins were living out the world of the Spenserian eclogue and of Virgil's *Georgics*. Indeed, connections may have been formed in Henry's mind, during the six years he spent with Matthew Herbert, between the tasks of the shepherd (not forgetting biblical echoes) and that of the poet, encouraging in him a view of poetry as care or healing. It must surely also have encouraged what Louis L. Martz described as Vaughan's particular genius: 'his individual apprehension of the divine presence in external nature and in the self'.[7] In a Latin poem, 'Venerabile Viro',[8] Henry addresses Matthew Herbert as his spiritual father, expressing the hope that what he owes his former tutor 'and always ... most cherished friend' may be indicated by 'my existence beyond the grave' – that is, by his survival through poetry.[9]

It seems certain that both Henry and Thomas entered Jesus College, Oxford, at 17, in 1638. This college was especially associated with Wales. There is no formal record of Henry's residence there, but he himself later explained to Aubrey that 'I stayed not att Oxford to take any degree, butt was sent to London, beinge then designed by my father for the study of the Law.'[10] Due to increasing civil unrest, Henry returned to Wales early in 1640 and took up a post in Brecon as secretary to the royalist judge, Sir Marmaduke Lloyd.

★

> *... for Marriage of all states*
> *Makes most unhappy, or most fortunates ...*
> 'Isaacs Marriage'

Civil War broke out in 1642. The Vaughan family, living a few miles from Brecon, was probably on visiting terms with the Price family at Brecon Priory, a monastic house serving by then as a private dwelling. It was probably here that Henry met his future wife, Catherine Wise, eldest daughter of a royalist Warwickshire family. 'Upon the Priorie Grove, His usuall Retyrement' (published in his first volume, *Poems*, in 1646) is thought to evoke the revelation to Catherine of Henry's love:

> Haile sacred shades! coole, leavie House!
> Chaste treasurer of all my vowes,
> And wealth ! on whose soft bosom layd
> My loves faire steps I first betrayd.

This early poem, set in what is still a charmingly wooded spot alongside a tributary of the Usk, is remarkable not only for its heartfelt quality but also for its sense of foreboding. It is as though the young lovers could only, in future, hope to 'kisse, and smile, and walke' in the 'shades' of Elysium. Certainly, Henry would have been all too aware, through his contacts both with the law and with the Price family, of growing national tensions and their implications for Catherine's and his own future. There is evidence that both Henry and Thomas enrolled in the Royalist cavalry under Sir Herbert Price. During the Civil War, it was with the Price family that King Charles stayed on his final journey through Wales. A letter survives from the king to his son Charles, written on 5 August 1645 from Brecon Priory not long before the king moved on and was, in due course, taken prisoner by Parliamentary forces.[11]

It seems likely that by the age of 25 Henry had married Catherine, and as his second volume of poems, *Olor Iscanus* ('The Swan of Usk'), was dedicated from '*Newton* by *Usk* this 17. of Decemb. 1647', the young family may by then have been living at Henry's family home of Newton. At the head of *Olor* Henry placed the Latin address 'Ad Posteros' in which he emphasizes that his times were 'harsh': 'I lived at a time when religious schism had divided and fragmented the English people, amongst the furies of priest and populace.'[12] The phrase 'I lived' suggests some doubt as to his own continued survival, as perhaps does the book's title, 'The Swan of Usk'.[13] Henry goes on to indicate that during this difficult period he has 'taught myself to endure' and has 'never desecrated what is holy with hideous violence, neither was my mind or my hand stained'. It seems typical of him that he should mention his mind before his hand, but just how we should understand this claim may be open to doubt. Thomas accounted as no sin the shedding of 'guilty blood', and that may then have been Henry's view also, although his views on war probably altered in later life, as did his view of himself as guiltless.[14] An elegy in *Olor* indicates that Henry was present in 1645 at the battle of Rowton Heath and presumably fought there. The elegy tells us with seeming approval that he caught sight of his friend 'R.W.' as 'his active hand / Drew bloud' before he vanished from sight.

★

> *Nor are wee so high-proofe, but griefe will find*
> *Through all our guards a way to wound the mind . . .*
> 'An Elegie on the death of Mr. *R. Hall*'

Despite the dedication, *Olor* remained unpublished until 1651. It seems possible that Henry's deepening insight into Christianity caused the delay, making him feel a need to let *Silex Scintillans* ('Flashing Flint') appear first, in 1650. Indeed, *Olor* is full of shadows. Although there is some suggestion in this, the poet's second collection, that Vaughan's appreciation of Christianity was deepening (especially in the translations from Boethius and Casimir, with their emphasis on the figure of the hermit), *Olor* is still full of classical references. Dr Peter Thomas has explored the revealing Orphic strains that are to be heard in these poems.[15]

Since the early days of Christianity, Orpheus had been viewed as a symbol of Christ, and Henry's fascination with 'holy *Orpheus*, Nature's *busy* child' may be traditional but is also personal. While he himself is composing beside the Usk, in a time of psychic dismemberment, he remembers Orpheus compiling 'deep *hymns*' beside the Hebrus,[16] and even imagines Orpheus being swept along in the Welsh river: 'I believe that the plaints of the dismembered Thracian move along your waters, and the lyre of the divine old man.'[17] Nevertheless, as we shall see, *Olor* contains no such overt and dramatic personal commitment to Christianity as is announced by the emblem at the head of *Silex*.[18]

The poems of *Olor* do however suggest that Vaughan felt himself to be facing traumatic experiences without adequate philosophical support. Stoicism and classical metaphors no longer meet the case. After finishing, presumably, at least the main body of *Olor* and while writing *Silex*, Vaughan clearly engaged in a sustained reading of the Bible. Was he now sensing a new order of reality, a deeper truth, accessible through the Bible? Certainly, he had taken as his mentor the great Christian poet George Herbert. Herbert (probably a distant relative) had died some 20 years earlier, leaving behind poems capable of teaching Vaughan a new approach both to metaphysics and to poetry. In the preface to an expanded edition of *Silex II*, published in 1655, Vaughan indicated the nature of his debt to Herbert: 'that blessed man, Mr. George Herbert, whose holy life and verse gained many pious converts (of whom I am the least)'. Herbert possessed, I think, a rather more even temperament than Vaughan's, and was of course living in a more settled society, but perhaps for that very reason he was the better able – through his poetic 'life after death' – to help the younger poet in his own search for emotional and spiritual balance.

The Civil War period was traumatic for the nation, and for Vaughan himself it was especially disastrous. Close friends were killed or lost their livings, his worldly expectations were shattered, and the death of his brother William, probably due to a war wound,[19] created in him a state of emotional and intellectual extremity. William died at home in Newton so that Henry was forced to witness his younger brother's death at close hand. The Civil War came to an end with King Charles's execution. Still only in his twenties, Henry seems to have given up any desire to make a name on the national stage.[20] He had chosen a 'cell'.

The poems Vaughan added to *Silex* for its enlarged edition (1655) seem less desperate than many of those in the first edition. They suggest an increasingly settled commitment to Christ and to the Christian community.

The emblem of a heart struck to flame and tears (perhaps blood) by the hand of God is replaced by a preface in which the poet takes stock of where writing *Silex I* and *II* has brought him. He considers the relevance of the direction he has taken, not just to his own physical and spiritual survival but to that of others, and to the validity of contemporary writing:

> ... he that desires to excel in this kind of *Hagiography*, or holy writing, must strive (by all means) for *perfection* and true *holyness*, that *a door may be opened to him in heaven*, Rev. 4.1. and then he will be able to write (with *Hierotheus* and holy *Herbert*) *A true Hymn*.
>
> To effect this in some measure, I have begged leave to communicate this my poor *Talent* to the *Church*, under the *protection* and *conduct* of her *glorious Head*; who (if he will vouchsafe to *own* it, and *go along* with it) can make it as useful now in the *publick*, as it hath been to me in *private*.

Vaughan is now a man whose sense of his proper role as poet – as the possessor of a biblical 'talent' (emphasized by italics) – is communal, in keeping with Welsh bardic tradition. The significance of Vaughan's attitude at this time may best be understood within the context provided by Evelyn Underhill's *Mysticism: The Nature and Development of Spiritual Consciousness*,[21] which contains several references to both Henry and Thomas. Especially relevant perhaps is Part Two, 'The Mystic Way', in which she explains that the 'systole-and- diastole motion of retreat as the preliminary to a return remains the true ideal of Christian Mysticism in its highest development'. Without wishing to claim that Henry Vaughan should be seen as a mystic in the fullest sense, I do think he experienced that same 'retreat' and 'return' – somewhat as the shaman, following his or her experience of personal disintegration, seeks to become a bridge for others between the material world and the world of the spirit.[22]

While *Silex II* was in preparation, Vaughan expected to die before the book appeared. As he remarks in the preface, the final poems in the volume might indeed lead a reader to think the book's appearance posthumous, especially if taken together with the 'solemn and accomplished *dress*' in which it appeared: 'For (indeed) *I was nigh unto death*, and am still at no great distance from it.' As the poet looks forward, he hopes that, if he does survive, he will 'flourish not with leaf only but with some fruit also'. This hope is supposed by some critics to hold a certain irony, in that after *Silex II* Vaughan published no more poetry until some 23 years later. But what if Vaughan was, by these words, indicating rather a redirection of his life's effort? There had been, after *Silex I*, the prose publications *The Mount of Olives or Solitary Devotions* (1652), *Flores Solitudinis* (1654), then *Hermetical Physic* (1655) – and, of course, the poems of *Silex II* – and, finally, in 1657 another prose work, *The Chemist's Key*. The prose publications of 1655 and 1657 perhaps indicate a turn towards medicine, and it seems possible that 'fruit' should be interpreted not as a reference to the production of more poetry but rather to Vaughan's future practice of a different kind of healing. He often saw the production of poetry as a form of natural growth, referring to verse as buds, leaves, shoots, flowers, a wreath,[23] yet there is in Vaughan's poetic output no certain reference to verse composition as 'fruit'. 'Unprofitablenes' does refer to 'fruit', and would be the exception if 'fruit' were taken to mean poetry. But we notice that even when Vaughan's poetic 'leaves' are again flourishing, he feels a need to offer something more: 'But, ah, my God! what fruit hast thou of this?' That 'But' is significant. It indicates that 'poor leaves' (poems) might, though flourishing, be seen as 'thankless weeds' unless they bear 'fruit'. Perhaps, for Vaughan in his maturity, healing by medical means grew quite directly out of healing by means of poetry – as fruit may come of such leaves and flowers as are truly worth a husbandman's care?[24] However that may be, it would be understandable if, having written his way through such an intense spiritual crisis, Vaughan would not wish to aim 'more at *verse*, than *perfection*' by continuing to write for the sake of a literary reputation or what he had so often castigated as 'self-ends'.[25]

An almost unbearable pain finds expression in 'As time one day by me did pass'. This may well be connected to the death of Vaughan's first wife, Catherine. Poems in *Silex II* refer to this loss. Remembering 'A beauty far more bright / Then the noons cloudless light', he ends the poem with these heart-wrenching lines:

> Sleep happy ashes! (blessed sleep!)
> While haplesse I still weep;
> Weep that I have out-liv'd
> My life, and unreliev'd
> Must (soul-lesse shadow!) so live on,
> Though life be dead, and my joys gone.

It may be that Catherine's death contributed to his illness, if this was of a psychological as well as physical nature. Perhaps the young widower's choice of Catherine's younger sister Elizabeth as his second wife suggests a certain 'turning in'. Certainly, during this time of grief, Elizabeth took charge of her three nieces and nephew. In due course, she too gave Henry three girls and a boy, so Newton Farm must again have become, as the years went by, a lively place.

It seems likely that Vaughan practised as a doctor for some 40 years, until shortly before his death on 23 April 1695. His only known publication in the intervening years is *Thalia Rediviva* ('The County Muse Revived'), a collection of poems most of which seem to have been written, or at least drafted, much earlier. It contains a few gems, such as 'Daphnis. An Elegiac *Eclogue*', probably written for William but adapted, after Thomas's death, to include (as I indicated earlier) memories of the twins' early life under Matthew Herbert's care at Llangattock:

> Here, when the careless world did sleep, have I
> In dark records and numbers noblie high
> The visions of our black, but brightest Bard
> From old *Amphion*'s mouth full often heard . . .

Henry and Elizabeth spent their last years together at Holly Bush Cottage, just along the road from Newton towards Brecon, above a bend in the Usk where, today, swans may often be seen. A stone carved with their initials

V

H   E

is to be found at the foot of Henry's grave behind the new Llansantfraed Church, erected in the late nineteenth century to replace the church Vaughan knew so well.[26]

It is strange to think how small a geographical area witnessed key events in Henry's life. No doubt this resulted not only from the negative effects of the Civil War on the poet's hopes of preferment but also from the positive influence of Welsh community life and the extraordinary beauty of the valley in which he was born. His early formative years were spent at Newton Farm and at nearby Llangattock. In Brecon he took his first job and joined Colonel Price's cavalry. In the Priory gardens he courted his first wife, Catherine. In the old white church of Llansantfraed, a few yards from Newton Farm, he must often have worshipped. There or in Brecon Cathedral he may have been married and had his children christened. Thomas, until the Puritans had him evicted, was rector of Llansantfraed.[27] At Newton, William and Catherine died, at Newton Henry's eight children were brought up and from Newton and Holly Bush Cottage Henry rode out to visit his patients in Brecon, Crickhowell and the surrounding area. Finally, he was still resident at Holly Bush Cottage when he died in his early seventies and was buried in a modest plot behind his local church.

I like to think that the pretty beehive bell tower of that church, added after Vaughan's death (whose weight eventually caused the building to collapse), might have been suggested to parishioners by one of their local poet's last published and most charming poems, 'The Bee', in which the believer is likened to a laden bee flying home to 'hive' with God.[28]

The Work

O! 'tis an easie thing
To write and sing;
But to write true, unfeigned verse
Is very hard! O God, disperse
These weights, and give my spirit leave
To act as well as to conceive!

O my God, hear my cry;
Or let me dye! ——
'Anguish'

For this anthology of Henry Vaughan's poems I have selected from all five of his collections. As we have seen, *Poems* appeared in 1646, when he was 25, *Silex Scintillans* in 1650, *Olor Iscanus* (dedicated in 1647) in 1651, and a much extended edition of *Silex Scintillans* (*Silex II*) in 1655. Finally, after a long pause, *Thalia Rediviva* appeared in 1678, when Vaughan was 57.

The period during which he wrote most intensively stretches from his early twenties to his early thirties. Over that short time both style and subject-matter were rapidly transformed by his experience of social and personal upheaval. One might characterize the first collection as the work of a talented but not original Cavalier poet. With *Olor Iscanus*, however, dark subjects intrude – the death of friends in the Civil War, death itself – along with a keener sense of impending personal doom. And yet, at the time, he may still have been in the state he describes in 'Repentance' (a poem in *Silex I*) when God's 'narrow way' seemed like an 'entrance to captivity':

Thy Promises but empty words
Which none but children heard, or taught.
This I believed ...

Indeed, certain poems in *Olor* seem to threaten a spiritual dead end. Maybe he is remembering this period when he writes, in *Silex I*: 'Dead I was, and deep in trouble'.[29]

★

. . . that which was formerly stone is now made flesh

From the moment of opening *Silex I* one is confronted by something quite new. Following George Herbert's example, Vaughan subtitles the collection 'sacred poems and private ejaculations' and symbolizes himself as author by a powerful visual emblem: a rocky heart struck to tears (perhaps to blood) by the right hand of God, but also to flame.

In the prefatory Latin poem 'Authoris (de se) Emblema', Vaughan uses the present tense and an emphatic repetition of 'now' to indicate that he has been overcome by an experience violent, redemptive, and above all still ongoing: 'I was a flint – deaf and silent . . . But You draw nearer and break that mass which is my rocky heart, and that which was formerly stone is now made flesh . . . By dying, I live again, and amidst the wreck of my worldly resources, I am now more rich.'[30] His commitment to Christianity has been gradual. Begun in earliest infancy,[31] belief has become for Vaughan in later life an irresistible necessity. God sought him, first with a 'holy murmur', but finally through extreme experience.

Compared with the poems of Vaughan's two earlier collections, the poems of *Silex I* are indeed more 'private', at times even confessional. And the nature of the struggle itself has changed. Rather than attempting to face with merely human equanimity the destruction by death of 'shoreless thoughts, vast tenter'd hope, / Ambitious dreams, *Aymes* of an Endless scope',[32] the poet's whole attention is now on the sacred power that 'bent the spheres'.[33] Style as well as subject matter have undergone a remarkable transformation; but then, in W. B. Yeats' words, when a poet struggles with style, 'it is myself that I remake'. Vaughan's desire is now to make contact with that God who is 'in all things, though invisibly',[34] and 'descry some glimpse of his great light'.[35] His pilgrimage is full of reverses. All too often he feels himself to be in a state of disintegration. 'Life without thee is loose and spills.'[36] At such times he feels himself to be 'crumbed', 'parcelled', 'unknit', scattered, 'loose', straying, mere sand or 'crumbled dust', and he associates this with being 'silent', unable to return praise to God – a 'speechless heap'. 'Loose, parcell'd hearts wil freeze'; in 'Love-Sick'[37] he begs that God's grace may come to him:

> ... at thy presence make these mountains flow,
> These mountains of cold Ice in me!

He feels himself to be like a bird which sees where it wishes to be but cannot reach the place: '*O that I were but where I see! / Is all the note within my Bush*'.[38]

★

> *A quickness, which my God hath kist.*

At other times, his heart is 'clean & steddy',[39] and then he is able to perceive at least 'thy edges, and thy bordering light'.[40] He experiences a joy which 'tramples on doubts and despair'.[41] 'False life' – 'a blinde / Self-posing state' – gives way to the true:

> Thou art a toylsom Mole, or less
> A moving mist
> But life is, what none can express,
> *A quickness, which my God hath kist.*
> ('Quickness')

In all this there is the unmistakable trace of turbulent personal struggles, during which the writing of 'true, unfeigned verse' played an essential and saving role. As he concludes in 'Man',

> Man is the shuttle, to whose winding quest
> And passage through these looms
> God order'd motion, but ordain'd no rest.

Intermittently perhaps, but with growing assurance as the experience is repeated, Vaughan senses that God remains in touch with him even when he himself feels far from God:

> Nay, at the very brink
> And edge of all
> When thou wouldst fall
> My *love-twist* held thee up, my *unseen link*.[42]

★

my unseen link

Indeed, the continuous but often hidden and secret presence of God is perhaps Vaughan's most essential perception; one which is deeply personal even if, in the mode of its expression, he may owe much to Christian hermeticism.[43] That wonderful poem 'The Sap' speaks of 'secret meals' and 'secret life', reminding us that

> There is at all times (though shut up) in you
> a powerful, rare dew,
> Which only grief and love extract . . .

Almost the last poem in *Silex I*, 'I walkt the other day', describes 'thy sacred way' as offering 'hid ascents' towards that day:

> Which breaks from thee
> Who art in all things, though invisibly . . .

In 'The Holy Communion' he widens this perspective, asserting that

> Nothing that is, or lives,
> But hath his Quicknings, and reprieves
> As thy hand opes, or shuts . . .

Such realizations contribute to the more stable emotions that are found in *Silex II*. In 'The Seed growing secretly' he goes further, for now he knows that such 'quicknings and reprieves' are always within reach because God, if never visible, is always present. And we may find them where we least expect them: in the words of a modern theologian and poet, 'those parts of our own individual experience that seem least pious or "together" may be the points at which we are exposed to God'.[44]

> Dear, secret *Greenness*! nurst below
> Tempests and windes, and winter-nights . . .

We find this same image of 'greenness' in Herbert, and Gerard Manley Hopkins, in 'God's Grandeur', writes: 'there lives the dearest freshness deep down things' – indicating the hidden presence of God's grace in even the direst of circumstances. Such thoughts suggest that while our own spiritual growth or that of others may not always be visible to us, it is always visible to God:

> Vex not, that but one sees thee grow,
> That *One* made all these lesser lights.

So, 'Bless thy secret growth'.

Perhaps Vaughan's most moving expression of this thought comes in 'The Agreement'. Here Vaughan remembers the time when he put his hand in the hand of his mentor, George Herbert, and made his commitment to God.[45] Foreseeing his own death, he suddenly accepts the final silence, because it will at last be the silence not of a 'speechless heap' – of one who 'had not one poor word to say' – but of faith:

> And when in death my speech is spent,
> O let that silence then prevail!
> O chase in that *cold calm* my foes,
> And hear my hearts last private throws!

> ★

> *Why if I see a rock or shelf,*
> *Shall I from thence cast down my self,*
> *Or by complying with the world,*
> *From the same precipice be hurl'd?*
> 'Childe-hood'

To fulfil his resolve, Vaughan had to turn away from dominant aspects of society in his (perhaps any) time. As the tone of *Poems* suggests, Vaughan knew only too well what it is to drift with the prevailing culture. But finally, pressed by public and private events, he came to realize that this culture encouraged in him only a 'false life' and that he must seek a new path. For Vaughan, 'my heart, my verse' must be as one,[46] so 'I will no longer Cobwebs spin, / I'm too much on the score'.[47] The emphasis placed on 'is' in the verse below (as if to contrast with some unspoken 'is not'), and the repetition of 'no more', convey how heartfelt this 'resolve' truly is:

> Follow the *Cry* no more: there is
> An ancient way
> All strewed with flowres, and happiness
> And fresh as *May*;
> There turn, and turn no more . . .
> ('The Resolve')

Some critics – surely not taking full account of the active role Vaughan had earlier played in the Civil War – have responded with disdain to early signs of this direction as they appear (though in a quite different context) in *Olor* ('To his retired Friend, an Invitation to *Brecknock*'):

> . . . let us
> 'Midst noise and War, of Peace, and mirth discusse.
> This portion thou wert born for: why should wee
> Vex at the times ridiculous miserie?
> An age that thus hath fool'd it selfe, and will
> (Spite of thy teeth and mine) persist so still.

This poem well indicates the tension Vaughan was under during the Civil War. His emphasis on the pleasures of drinking in convivial company might be a way of expressing either hedonism or undaunted resistance.[48] In any case, I doubt if it is to understood as escapist irresponsibility. Wondering what has prevented his friend from coming to see him, Vaughan jokingly suggests that, had his friend been a bachelor, a 'monastic mind' or a 'nymph to visit' might be causes of his absence. After exploring the latter possibility with some gusto, he returns to the former:

> Or is't thy pietie? for who can tell
> But thou may'st prove devout, and love a Cell,
> And (like a Badger) with attentive looks
> In the dark hole sit rooting up of books.
> Quick Hermit! what a peacefull Change hadst thou
> Without the noise of *haire-cloth*, *Whip*, or *Vow*?
> But is there no redemption?

Perhaps such thoughts, though humorously handled here, are indicative (somewhat as a Freudian slip might be) of the way Vaughan was already beginning to see his own options.

★

> *Open my desolate rooms* . . .
> 'Dressing'

A poem in *Silex I* tells us that it was by no means easy for Vaughan to choose a 'cell'. In 'Misery' he addresses the Lord thus:

> . . . now thy grace
> (I know it wel,) fils all the place;

I sit with thee by this new light,
And for that hour th'art my delight,
No man can more the world despise
Or thy great mercies better prize.
I School my Eys, and strictly dwel
Within the Circle of my Cel,
That Calm and silence are my Joys
Which to thy peace are but meer noise.
At length I feel my head to ake,
My fingers Itch, and burn to take
Some new Imployment, I begin
To swel and fome and fret within.
   'The Age, the present times are not
   To snudge in, and embrace a Cot
   Action and bloud now get the game . . .'

This account is all too clearly autobiographical. Vaughan leaves no doubt that 'with the bloud of all my soul' he is struggling to accept a new and unfamiliar way of life. Perhaps this is why the image of desolate interiors recurs so persistently. In 'Dressing', for instance, he begs God to

                    . . . touch with one Coal
   My frozen heart; and with thy secret key

   Open my desolate rooms; my gloomie Brest
   With thy cleer fire refine, burning to dust
   These dark Confusions, that within me nest . . .

and in 'The Match' he asks him to

   Settle my *house*, and shut out all distractions
               That may unknit
      My heart, and thee planted in it . . .

It is Vaughan's habit to signal by means of italics that words have a special as well as an obvious meaning. 'House' here probably refers to 'the House of Light', that heavenly 'Aula Lucis' often referred to by his brother Thomas.[49] Similar references appear elsewhere in Henry's poems. For instance, there is within the cocks in 'Cock-crowing' a light that answers to that of the sun and of heaven: 'their little grain expelling night / So shines and sings, as if it knew / The path unto the house of light', the abode of the 'Father of lights'. Clearly, their 'little grain' is akin to the 'seed' of spiritual understanding or 'light' that dwells in a human being, as is made clear a few lines later in the same poem:

> Seeing thy seed abides in me,
> Dwell thou in it, and I in thee.

This metaphor, drawn of course from the Bible, also signals that it will be in nature that Vaughan finds the solution to his 'snudged' state. His meditative 'hour', spent walking out of doors, becomes a vital aspect of his new life. He seems to love especially his morning walks, for '*Mornings* are *Mysteries*',[50] emblems of genesis that also seem to presage the coming of Christ, the dawn of a totally new day:

> The fields are long since white, and I
> With earnest groans for freedom cry,
> My fellow-creatures too say, *Come!*
> And stones, though speechless, are not dumb.
> ('The day of Judgement')[51]

When he seeks to describe that time 'When first I saw true beauty'[52] it is to nature that he turns for adequate metaphors. In a passage that is bound to remind the modern reader of the opening of Wordsworth's 'Tintern Abbey' he writes of the effect this moment of spiritual realization had on him, and continues to have as he remembers it in harsher times:

> I am so warm'd now by this glance on me,
> That, midst all storms I feel a Ray of thee;
> So have I known some beauteous *Paisage* rise
> In suddain flowres and arbours to my Eies,
> And in the depth and dead of winter bring
> To my Cold thoughts a lively sense of spring.

But it is not a matter only of metaphors. As Louis L. Martz remarked, Vaughan's particular genius did indeed lie in 'his individual apprehension of the divine presence in external nature and in the self'.[53]

★

> ... *all is hurl'd*
> *In sacred Hymnes, and Order, The great Chime*
> *And Symphony of nature.*

One of the most beautiful of Vaughan's poems is 'The Morning-watch'. It records a morning on which he woke with the sense of 'dew' having fallen on him during the hours of darkness. Because of this, he feels in tune with awakening nature: 'with what flowres, / And shoots of glory, my soul breakes, and buds!'

> In what Rings,
> And *Hymning Circulations* the quick world
> Awakes, and sings;
> The rising winds,
> And falling springs,
> Birds, beasts, all things
> Adore him in their kinds.
> Thus all is hurl'd
> In sacred *Hymnes*, and *Order*, The great *Chime*
> And *Symphony* of nature. Prayer is
> The world in tune ...

Here the adult seems to have regained the insight of the child who had, with such miraculous ease, 'felt through all this fleshly dresse / Bright shootes of everlastingnesse'.[54] It is that lost capacity which Vaughan seems to have regained, from time to time at least, on his spiritual pilgrimage. But how difficult it was to attain is made clear in 'Vanity of Spirit'. That poem records a very different experience of morning. There is here no sense of sacred 'dew', but rather of intense intellectual struggle: 'Quite spent with thoughts I left my Cell, and lay / Where a shrill spring tun'd to the early day.' Vaughan is, as before, sensitive to the natural sounds of morning, but as for himself: 'I ... gron'd to know / Who gave the Clouds so brave a bow.' This time, the pursuit of knowledge is not through any intuitive apprehension of divine presence but through an attempt to force nature to give up her divine secrets:

> I summon'd nature: pierc'd through all her store,
> Broke up some seales, which none had touch'd before,
> Her wombe, her bosome, and her head
> Where all her secrets lay a bed
> I rifled quite ...

Only within himself does he find 'Traces, and sounds of a strange kind': 'Here of this mighty spring, I found some drills, / And Ecchoes beaten from th' eternall hills . . .'

The poem ends on the thought that death would be welcome if by means of it he could at last 'find out / The mystery' and '*buy / But one half glaunce*' of divine truth. But the title 'Vanity of Spirit' is significant, as is the order in which these two poems are placed in *Silex I*. Of course we do not know the sequence in which the poems were written, but the similar settings and the fact that in *Silex I* Vaughan placed 'Vanity of Spirit' before 'The Morning-watch' suggest that by the time the published order of the poems was decided on, Vaughan had realized that his path to 'regeneration' or enlightenment could not be the one taken by his brother. Reading the works of these twins, Henry the poet-doctor and Thomas the priest-alchemist, there can be no doubt how similar were their aims, nor how different were the paths they would eventually choose to follow.

For Henry, the sense of being a part of nature rather than a student of it became crucial. Poem after poem in *Silex I* indicates how intimately he felt other living creatures and even inanimate things to be in touch with the deity and true 'fellows' of humanity. As we saw earlier, the cock crowing in the morning held a 'grain' of God's light. Elsewhere the poet encourages his reader to rise before daybreak to

> Walk with thy fellow-creatures: note the *hush*
> And *whispers* amongst them. There's not a *Spring*,
> Or *Leafe* but hath his *Morning-hymn*; Each *Bush*
> And *Oak* doth know *I AM* ; canst thou not sing?
> ('Rules *and* Lessons')

*

> *O knowing, glorious spirit! when*
> *Thou shalt restore trees, beasts and men,*
> *When thou shalt make all new again,*
> *Destroying onely death and pain,*
> *Give him amongst thy works a place,*
> *Who in them lov'd and sought thy face!*
> 'The Book'

Vaughan's sense of humankind as part of nature comes out clearly in 'The Book'. The humblest components of his Bible – the seed that produced the grass that went to make linen and then paper, the tree whose wood provided a cover, the beast whose skin was stretched over it – are seen as sacred beings, known to God before and after their death: 'Thou knew'st and saw'st them all and though / Now scatter'd thus, dost know them so'. His own human dust will remain known to God, all the more because in life he sought God's face in the natural world. I find this a profoundly attractive way of expressing the belief that, whatever secular interpretations may suggest, 'no thing can to *Nothing* fall'.

> For a preserving spirit doth still passe
> Untainted through this Masse . . .
> ('Resurrection and Immortality')

In Vaughan's own words on another occasion,

> So some strange thoughts transcend our wonted theams,
> And into glory peep.
> ('They are all gone into the world of light!')

The spiritual direction taken by Henry Vaughan combines sparkling intellectuality with preparedness to take on the limitations of human understanding and language – a willingness to accept that 'Love only can with quick accesse / Unlock the way',[55] and that it may sometimes be wise 'to carry, not search mysteries'.[56]

★

> . . . that's best
> *Which is not fixt, but flies, and flowes* . . .
> 'Affliction'

In Vaughan's mature work there is an acceptance of, even rejoicing in, change. He senses (as we have seen) that whatever exists, or ever has existed, is eternally sustained by God's 'preserving spirit'. Perhaps that is why the style Vaughan finds for many of the finest poems in *Silex Scintillans* also 'flies, and flowes'. Louis L. Martz has described the essential difference between Ignatian and Augustinian meditation:

> Ignatian meditation is . . . a precise, tightly articulated method, moving from the images that comprise the composition of place into the threefold sequence of the powers of the soul, memory, understanding and will, and from there into the affections and resolutions of the aroused will. But in Augustinian meditation, there is no such precise method; there is, rather, an intuitive groping back

into regions of the soul that lie beyond sensory memories. The three faculties of the soul are all used, but with an effect of simultaneous action, for with Augustine the aroused will is using the understanding to explore the memory, with the aim of apprehending more clearly and loving more fervently the ultimate source of the will's arousal.[57]

Vaughan's best poems seem to me to progress in an essentially Augustinian manner. They do indeed give the impression of someone finding his way by 'intuitive groping', words and experience coming together simultaneously in a molten flow, provisional and for that very reason all the more vibrant.[58] The great American poet Wallace Stevens describes a poem of this kind as 'the poem of the mind in the act of finding / What will suffice': 'It has to be living . . . It has to face the time . . . It has to think about war / And it has to find what will suffice'.[59] In this sense, Vaughan is remarkably modern. His sense of form is also, I suspect, influenced by Welsh poetry. Gwyn Williams, in his study of Welsh poetry, *The Burning Tree*, provides the following description:

> The absence of a centred design, of an architectural quality, is not a weakness in old Welsh poetry, but results quite reasonably from a specific view of composition. English and most Western European creative activity has been conditioned by the inheritance from Greece and Rome of the notion of a central point of interest in a poem, a picture or a play, a nodal region to which everything leads and upon which everything depends. The dispersed nature of the thematic splintering of Welsh poetry is not due to failure to follow this classical convention. [The Welsh poets] were not trying to write poems that would read like Greek temples or even Gothic cathedrals but, rather, like stone circles or the contour-following rings of the forts from which they fought, with hidden ways slipping from one ring to another.[60]

In reading Vaughan, we must often be prepared to 'slip from one ring to another' but the experience his poetry is capable of providing is all the more able to catch us unawares and move us deeply. Familiar though a poem may have become through the years, we suddenly understand some phrase in a new light and so intensely that tears arise, as if in response to a phrase in music. At these moments, over three hundred years vanish away and we hear the voice of a dear friend.

Notes

1 All the poems selected for this volume are taken from L. C. Martin (ed.), *Henry Vaughan: Poetry and Selected Prose*, second edition, Oxford University Press, 1963.

2 From 'Ad Posteros'. Translation from Alan Rudrum, *Henry Vaughan: The Complete Poems (CP)*, Penguin Classics, 1976, p. 63.

3 See F. E. Hutchinson, *Henry Vaughan: A Life and Interpretation (HV)*, Clarendon Press, 1947, p. 14.

4 From *Euphrates, Or the Waters of the East*, 1655, in *The Works of Thomas Vaughan*, ed. Alan Rudrum, Clarendon Press, 1984, p. 521. Alchemy was 'the chemistry of the middle ages and sixteenth century' (OED) but many scientists and medical men of the seventeenth century remained practitioners. While some alchemists were interested in the transmutation of baser metals into gold, others mainly took an interest in healing, as did Thomas Vaughan, seeking the panacea or universal remedy.

5 See p. 178.

6 In *Timeslips*, Carcanet New Press, 1997.

7 Louis L. Martz, *Henry Vaughan*, Oxford Poetry Library, 1995, p. xi. 'Vanity of Spirit' is relevant here.

8 Translation from Rudrum, *CP*, p. 131.

9 See the Preface to *Silex II* for Vaughan's mature thoughts on the implications of personal survival in poetry.

10 See Hutchinson, *HV*, p. 687.

11 See Hutchinson, *HV*, p. 64.

12 Rudrum, *CP*, pp. 63–4.

13 In *Silex II* there is a reference, in the last line of 'Jesus Weeping' (Martin, p. 505), to a grief that will send the poet '(*Swan-like*) singing home'.

14 See, for example, 'The men of War', Martin, p. 517.

15 Dr Peter Thomas offers a valuable exploration of Orphic elements in Vaughan's work in 'Henry Vaughan, Orpheus, and the Empowerment of Poetry', in the Festschrift volume in honour of Alan Rudrum, forthcoming from Delaware Press (essays on Vaughan and Milton).

16 'To the River Isca'.

17 Rudrum, *CP*, p. 130.

18 See 'Authoris (de se) Emblema' and facing illustration in Martin, pp. 386–7. See also 'The Tempest', Martin, p. 462. The significance of both poem and emblem is discussed more fully later on.

19 See Hutchinson, *HV*, p. 97. He quotes Thomas Vaughan's comment that his brother William died 'upon a . . . glorious employment'.

20 See 'The Proffer'.

21 Oneworld Publications, 1993.

22 See further discussion of this aspect of Vaughan's experience in my 'Rereading Henry Vaughan's "Distraction" ', *Scintilla 1* (1997).

23 See, for example, 'Disorder *and* Frailty', and 'The Wreath' (Martin p. 539).

24 See related images deployed in John 15.1–6.

25 The phrase 'more at *verse*, than *perfection*' is applied by Vaughan to any poet who 'takes pen in hand, out of no other consideration, then to be seen in print' (Preface, *Silex II*).

26 By the late 1800s the church Vaughan knew had fallen into a ruinous condition. The new church retains the original font and the porch stoup.

27 See Hutchinson, *HV*, pp. 91–5.

28 The details of Henry's father's will are given in Hutchinson, *HV*, pp.16–17. The executors of Thomas Vaughan's will (1658) are given as Thomas Powell, David Maddocks and John Watkins. It is interesting to note that the bell for which the beehive bell tower was erected after Vaughan's death is inscribed as follows: 'William Powell, David Maddocks, CP Church Wardens 1676' (see *Llansantffraed-Juxta-Usk*, a pamphlet published in 1985 to celebrate the centenary of the new church). Hutchinson tells us that the David Maddocks who acted as Thomas Vaughan's executor did not die till 1685, so he may well be the David Maddocks whose name is inscribed on the bell, and may have had a voice in deciding the shape of the bell tower. And William Powell may have been related to Thomas Powell. The date of the bell tower is uncertain, however: Theophilus Jones' *History of Brecknock-shire* (1805–9) gives it as 1690, but Lord Glanusk in his edition of Theophilus Jones suggests that the large circular bell-turret dates from the eighteenth century.

29 'The Holy Communion'.

30 Rudrum, *CP*, p. 137.

31 See 'To the Holy Bible'.

32 'The Charnel-house'.

33 'Vanity of Spirit'.

34 'I walkt the other day'.

35 'Vanity of Spirit'.

36 'The Seed growing secretly'.

37 Martin, p. 493.

38 'The Pilgrimage', Martin, p. 464.

39 'The Feast', Martin, p. 534.

40 'Childe-hood'.

41 'The Quere'. The title of this poem is 'The Queer' in Martin.

42 'Retirement', *Silex I*, Martin, p. 462.

43 See a detailed discussion of hermeticism as it relates to the Vaughans' writings in Alan Rudrum, *Henry Vaughan*, Writers of Wales, University of Wales Press, 1981. The OED gives this short description of the adjective 'hermetic': 'Pertaining to Hermes Trismegistus, and the writings ascribed to him . . . Hence, relating to or dealing with occult science, esp. alchemy.'

44 Rowan Williams in *Ponder These Things*, Canterbury Press, 2002, p. 49.

45 'The Match'.

46 'Disorder *and* Frailty', Martin, p. 444.

47 'Idle Verse', Martin, p. 446.

48 See also 'To my worthy friend Master T. Lewes'.

49 See, for example, 'Aula Lucis' (1652), in *The Works of Thomas Vaughan*, ed. Alan Rudrum, Clarendon Press, 1984, p. 451.

50 'Rules *and* Lessons'.

51 Martin, p. 530.

52 'Mount of Olives'.

53 Martz, *Henry Vaughan*, p. xi.

54 'The Retreate'.

55 'The Showre'.

56 'The Ass', Martin, p. 518.

57 See Louis L. Martz, 'Henry Vaughan: The Man Within', *Publications of the Modern Language Association of America*, 78 (1961), reprinted in *Essential Articles for the Study of Henry Vaughan*, ed. Alan Rudrum, Archon Books, 1987.

58 There is further discussion of this aspect of Vaughan's style in my 'Re-reading Henry Vaughan's "Distraction"', *Scintilla* 1 (1997).

59 In 'Of Modern Poetry', *The Collected Poems of Wallace Stevens*, Faber and Faber, 1945, p. 239.

60 *The Burning Tree: Poems from the First Thousand Years of Welsh Verse*, selected and translated by Gwyn Williams, Faber and Faber, 1956, from the Preface.

UPON THE PRIORIE GROVE,
His usuall Retyrement

Haile sacred shades! coole, leavie House!
Chaste Treasurer of all my vowes,
And wealth! on whose soft bosome layd
My loves faire steps I first betrayd:
　　Henceforth no melancholy flight,
No sad wing, or hoarse bird of Night,
Disturbe this Aire, no fatall throate
Of Raven, or Owle, awake the Note
Of our laid Eccho, no voice dwell
Within these leaves, but *Philomel*.
The poisonous Ivie here no more
His false twists on the Oke shall score,
Only the Woodbine here may twine,
As th' Embleme of her Love, and mine;
The Amorous Sunne shall here convey
His best beames, in thy shades to play;
The active ayre, the gentlest show'rs,
Shall from his wings raine on thy flowers;
And the Moone from her dewie lockes
Shall decke thee with her brightest drops:
What ever can a fancie move,
Or feed the eye; Be on this Grove;
　　And when at last the Winds, and Teares
Of Heaven, with the consuming yeares,
Shall these greene curles bring to decay,
And cloathe thee in an aged Gray:
(If ought a Lover can foresee;
Or if we Poets, Prophets be)
From hence transplanted, thou shalt stand
A fresh Grove in th' Elysian Land;
Where (most blest paire!) as here on Earth
Thou first didst eye our growth, and birth;
So there againe, thou 'lt see us move

In our first Innocence, and Love:
And in thy shades, as now, so then,
Wee'le kisse, and smile, and walke agen.

From *Olor Iscanus*

To the River *Isca*

When *Daphne's* Lover here first wore the *Bayes*,
Eurotas secret streams heard all his *Layes*.
And holy *Orpheus*, Natures *busie* Child
By headlong *Hebrus* his deep *Hymns* Compil'd.
Soft *Petrarch* (thaw'd by *Laura's* flames) did weep
On *Tybers* banks, when she (*proud fair!*) cou'd sleep;
Mosella boasts *Ausonius*, and the *Thames*
Doth murmure SYDNEYS *Stella* to her *streams*,
While *Severn* swoln with *Joy* and *sorrow*, wears
Castara's smiles mixt with fair *Sabrin's* tears.
Thus *Poets* (like the *Nymphs*, their *pleasing themes*)
Haunted the *bubling Springs* and *gliding streams*,
And *happy banks!* whence such *fair flowres* have sprung,
But happier those where they have *sate* and *sung!*
Poets (like *Angels*) where they once appear
Hallow the *place*, and each succeeding year
Adds *rev'rence* to't, such as at length doth give
This aged faith, *That there their Genii live.*
Hence th'*Ancients* say, That, from this *sickly aire*
They passe to *Regions* more *refin'd* and *faire*,
To *Meadows* strow'd with *Lillies* and the *Rose*,
And *shades* whose *youthfull green* no *old age* knowes,
Where all in *white* they walk, discourse, and Sing
Like Bees *soft murmurs*, or a *Chiding Spring*.
      But *Isca*, whensoe'r those *shades* I see,
And thy *lov'd Arbours* must no more *know* me,
When I am layd to *rest* hard by thy *streams*,
And my *Sun sets*, where first it *sprang* in beams,

I'le leave behind me such a *large, kind light*,
As shall *redeem* thee from *oblivious night*,
And in these *vowes* which (living yet) I pay
Shed such a *Previous* and *Enduring Ray*,
As shall from age to age thy *fair name* lead
'Till *Rivers* leave to *run*, and *men* to *read*.
First, may all *Bards* born after me
(When I am *ashes*) sing of thee!
May thy *green banks* and *streams* (or none)
Be both their *Hill* and *Helicon*;
May *Vocall Groves* grow there, and all
The *shades* in them *Propheticall*,
Where (laid) men shall more *faire truths* see
Than *fictions* were of *Thessalie*.
May thy gentle *Swains* (like *flowres*)
Sweetly spend their *Youthfull houres*,
And thy *beauteous Nymphs* (like *Doves*)
Be *kind* and *faithfull* to their *Loves*;
Garlands, and *Songs*, and *Roundelayes*,
Mild, dewie *nights*, and Sun-shine *dayes*,
The *Turtles voyce, Joy* without *fear*,
Dwell on thy *bosome* all the year!
May the *Evet* and the *Tode*
Within thy Banks have no abode,
Nor the *wilie, winding Snake*
Her *voyage* through thy *waters* make.
In all thy *Journey* to the *Main*
No *nitrous Clay*, nor *Brimstone-vein*
Mixe with thy *streams*, but may they passe
Fresh as the *aire*, and cleer as *Glasse*,
And where the *wandring Chrystal* treads
Roses shall *kisse*, and *Couple* heads.
The *factour-wind* from far shall bring
The *Odours* of the *Scatter'd* Spring,
And *loaden* with the rich *Arreare*,
Spend it in *Spicie whispers* there.

No *sullen heats*, nor *flames* that are
Offensive, and *Canicular*,
Shine on thy *Sands*, nor *pry* to see
Thy *Scalie, shading familie*,
But *Noones* as mild as *Hesper's* rayes,
Or the first *blushes* of fair dayes.
What *gifts* more *Heav'n* or *Earth* can adde
With all those *blessings* be thou *Clad*!

      Honour, Beautie,
      Faith and *Dutie,*
      Delight and *Truth,*
      With *Love* and *Youth*

Crown all about thee! And what ever *Fate*
Impose else-where, whether the graver state,
Or some toye else, may those *lowd, anxious Cares*
For *dead* and *dying things* (the Common *Wares*
And *showes* of time) ne'r break thy *Peace*, nor make
Thy *repos'd Armes* to a new warre *awake*!

      But *Freedome, safety, Joy* and *blisse*
      United in one loving *kisse*
      Surround thee quite, and *stile* thy borders
      The Land redeem'd from all disorders!

The Charnel-house

Blesse me! what damps are here? how stiffe an aire?
Kelder of mists, a second *Fiats* care,
Frontspeece o'th' grave and darkness, a Display
Of ruin'd man, and the disease of day;
Leane, bloudless shamble, where I can descrie
Fragments of men, Rags of Anatomie;
Corruptions ward-robe, the transplantive bed
Of mankind, and th'Exchequer of the dead.
How thou arrests my sense? how with the sight
My *Winter'd* bloud growes stiffe to all delight?
Torpedo to the Eye! whose least glance can
Freeze our wild lusts, and rescue head-long man;
Eloquent silence! able to Immure
An *Atheists* thoughts, and blast an *Epicure.*
Were I a *Lucian,* Nature in this dresse
Would make me wish a Saviour, and Confesse.
    Where are you shoreless thoughts, vast tenter'd hope,
Ambitious dreams, *Aymes* of an Endless scope,
Whose stretch'd Excesse runs on a string too high
And on the rack of self-extension dye?
Chameleons of state, Aire-monging band,
Whose breath (like Gun-powder) blowes up a land,
Come see your dissolution, and weigh
What a loath'd nothing you shall be one day,
As th' Elements by Circulation passe
From one to th'other, and that which first was
Is so again, so 'tis with you; The grave
And Nature but Complott, what the one gave,
The other takes; Think then, that in this bed
There sleep the Reliques of as proud a head
As stern and subtill as your own, that hath
Perform'd, or forc'd as much, whose tempest-wrath
Hath levell'd Kings with slaves, and wisely then
Calme these high furies, and descend to men;

Thus *Cynus* tam'd the *Macedon*, a tombe
Checkt him, who thought the world too straight a Room.
   Have I obey'd the *Powers* of a face,
A beauty able to undoe the Race
Of easie man? I look but here, and strait
I am Inform'd, the lovely Counterfeit
Was but a smoother Clay. That famish'd slave
Begger'd by wealth, who starves that he may save,
Brings hither but his sheet; Nay, th'*Ostrich-man*
That feeds on *steele* and *bullet*, he that can
Outswear his *Lordship*, and reply as tough
To a kind word, as if his tongue were *Buffe*,
Is *Chap*-faln here, wormes without wit, or fear
Defie him now, death hath disarm'd the *Bear*.
Thus could I run o'r all the pitteous score
Of erring men, and having done meet more,
Their shuffled *Wills*, abortive, vain *Intents*,
Phantastick *humours*, perillous *Ascents*,
False, empty *honours*, traiterous *delights*,
And whatsoe'r a blind Conceit Invites;
But these and more which the weak vermins swell,
Are Couch'd in this Accumulative Cell
Which I could scatter; But the grudging Sun
Calls home his beams, and warns me to be gone,
Day leaves me in a double night, and I
Must bid farewell to my sad library.
Yet with these notes. Henceforth with thought of thee
I'le season all succeeding Jollitie,
Yet damn not mirth, nor think too much is fit,
Excesse hath no *Religion*, nor *Wit*,
But should wild bloud swell to a lawless strain
One Check from thee shall *Channel* it again.

To his retired friend, an Invitation to *Brecknock*

Since last wee met, thou and thy horse (my dear,)
Have not so much as drunk, or litter'd here,
I wonder, though thy self be thus deceast,
Thou hast the spite to Coffin up thy beast;
Or is the *Palfrey* sick, and his rough hide
With the penance of *One Spur* mortifide?
Or taught by thee (like *Pythagoras's Oxe*)
Is then his master grown more *Orthodox*?
What ever 'tis, a sober cause't must be
That thus long bars us of thy Companie.
The Town believes thee lost, and didst thou see
But half her suffrings, now distrest for thee,
Thou'ldst swear (like *Rome*) her foule, polluted walls
Were sackt by *Brennus*, and the salvage *Gaules*.
Abominable face of things! here's noise
Of bang'd Mortars, blew Aprons, and Boyes,
Pigs, Dogs, and Drums, with the hoarse hellish notes
Of politickly-deafe Usurers throats,
With new fine *Worships*, and the old cast *teame*
Of Justices vext with the *Cough*, and *flegme*.
Midst these the *Crosse* looks sad, and in the *Shire-*
-Hall furs of an old *Saxon Fox* appear,
With brotherly Ruffs and Beards, and a strange sight
Of high Monumentall Hats ta'ne at the fight
Of *Eighty eight*; while ev'ry *Burgesse* foots
The mortall *Pavement* in eternall boots.

Hadst thou been batc'lour, I had soon divin'd
Thy Close retirements, and Monastick mind,
Perhaps some Nymph had been to visit, or
The beauteous Churle was to be waited for,
And like the *Greek*, e'r you the sport would misse
You stai'd, and stroak'd the *Distaffe* for a kisse.
But in this age, when thy coole, settled bloud
Is ty'd t'one flesh, and thou almost grown good,

I know not how to reach the strange device,
Except (*Domitian* like) thou murther'st flyes;
Or is't thy pietie? for who can tell
But thou may'st prove devout, and love a Cell,
And (like a Badger) with attentive looks
In the dark hole sit rooting up of books.
Quick Hermit! what a peacefull Change hadst thou
Without the noise of *haire-cloth, Whip*, or *Vow*?
But is there no redemption? must there be
No other penance but of liberty?
Why two months hence, if thou continue thus
Thy memory will scarce remain with us,
The Drawers have forgot thee, and exclaim
They have not seen thee here since *Charles* his raign,
Or if they mention thee, like some old man
That at each word inserts – Sir, *as I can
Remember* – So the *Cyph'rers* puzzle mee
With a dark, cloudie character of thee.
That (certs!) I fear thou wilt be lost, and wee
Must ask the *Fathers* e'r 't be long for thee.
      Come! leave this sullen state, and let not Wine
And precious Witt lye dead for want of thine,
Shall the dull *Market-land-lord* with his *Rout*
Of sneaking Tenants durtily swill out
This harmless liquor? shall they knock and beat
For Sack, only to talk of *Rye* and *Wheat*?
O let not such prepost'rous tipling be
In our *Metropolis*, may I ne'r see
Such *Tavern-sacrilege*, nor lend a line
To weep the *Rapes* and *Tragedy* of wine!
Here lives that *Chimick*, quick fire which betrayes
Fresh Spirits to the bloud, and warms our layes,
I have reserv'd 'gainst thy approach a Cup
That were thy Muse stark dead, shall raise her up,
And teach her yet more Charming words and skill
Than ever *Cælia, Chloris, Astrophil*,

Or any of the Thredbare names Inspir'd
Poore riming lovers with a *Mistris* fir'd.
Come then! and while the slow Isicle hangs
At the stiffe thatch, and Winters frosty pangs
Benumme the year, blith (as of old) let us
'Midst noise and War, of Peace, and mirth discusse.
This portion thou wert born for: why should wee
Vex at the times ridiculous miserie?
An age that thus hath fool'd it selfe, and will
(Spite of thy teeth and mine) persist so still.
Let's sit then at this *fire*, and while wee steal
A Revell in the Town, let others seal,
Purchase or Cheat, and who can, let them pay,
Till those black deeds bring on the darksome day;
Innocent spenders wee! a better use
Shall wear out our short Lease, and leave th'obtuse
Rout to their *husks*; They amid their bags at best
Have cares in *earnest,* wee care for a *Jest.*

An Elegie on the death of Mr. *R. W.* slain in the late unfortunate differences at *Routon* Heath, neer *Chester*, 1645

I am Confirm'd, and so much wing is given
To my wild thoughts, that they dare strike at heav'n.
A full years griefe I struggled with, and stood
Still on my sandy hopes uncertain good,
So loth was I to yeeld, to all those fears
I still oppos'd thee, and denyed my tears.
But thou art gone! and the untimely losse
Like that one day, hath made all others Crosse.
Have you seen on some Rivers flowrie brow
A well-built *Elme*, or stately *Cedar* grow,
Whose Curled tops gilt with the Morning-ray
Becken'd the Sun, and whisperd to the day,
When unexpected from the angry *North*
A fatall sullen whirle-wind sallies forth,
And with a full-mouth'd blast rends from the ground
The *Shady twins*, which rushing scatter round
Their sighing leafes, whilst overborn with strength,
Their trembling heads bow to a prostrate length;
So forc'd fell he; So Immaturely Death
Stifled his able heart and active breath.
The world scarce knew him yet, his early Soule
Had but new-broke her day, and rather stole
A sight, than gave one; as if subt'ly she
Would learn our stock, but hide his treasurie.
His years (should time lay both his *Wings* and *glasse*
Unto his charge) could not be summ'd (alas!)
To a full *score*; Though in so short a span
His riper thoughts had purchas'd more of man
Than all those worthless livers, which yet quick,
Have quite outgone their own *Arithmetick*.
He seiz'd perfections, and without a dull
And mossie *gray* possess'd a solid skull,

No Crooked knowledge neither, nor did he
Wear the friends name for Ends and policie,
And then lay't by; As those *lost Youths* of th'stage
Who only flourish'd for the *Play's* short age
And then retir'd, like *Jewels* in each part
He wore his friends, but chiefly at his heart.
   Nor was it only in this he did excell,
His equall valour could as much, as well.
He knew no *fear* but of his *God*; yet durst
No injurie, nor (as some have) e'r purs't
The sweat and tears of others, yet would be
More forward in a royall gallantrie
Than all those vast pretenders, which of late
Swell'd in the ruines of their King and State.
He weav'd not *Self-ends*, and the *Publick* good
Into one piece, nor with the peoples bloud
Fill'd his own veins; In all the doubtfull way
Conscience and *Honour* rul'd him. O that day
When like the *Fathers* in the *Fire* and *Cloud*
I mist thy face! I might in ev'ry *Crowd*
See Armes like thine, and men advance, but none
So neer to lightning mov'd, nor so fell on.
Have you observ'd how soon the nimble *Eye*
Brings th' *Object* to *Conceit*, and doth so vie
Performance with the *Soul*, that you would swear
The *Act* and *apprehension* both lodg'd there,
Just so mov'd he: like *shott* his active hand
Drew bloud, e'r well the foe could understand.
But here I lost him. Whether the last turn
Of thy few sands call'd on thy hastie urn,
Or some fierce rapid fate (hid from the Eye)
Hath hurl'd thee Pris'ner to some distant skye
I cannot tell, but that I doe believe
Thy Courage such as scorn'd a base Reprieve.
What ever 'twas, whether that day thy breath
Suffer'd a *Civill* or the *Common* death,

Which I doe most suspect, and that I have
Fail'd in the *glories* of so known a grave,
Though thy lov'd ashes misse me, and mine Eyes
Had no acquaintance with thy Exequies,
Nor at the last farewell, torn from thy sight
On the *Cold sheet* have fix'd a *sad delight*,
Yet what e'r pious hand (in stead of mine)
Hath done this office to that dust of thine,
And till thou rise again from thy low bed
Lent a Cheap pillow to thy quiet head,
Though but a private *turffe*, it can do more
To keep thy name and memory in store
Than all those *Lordly fooles* which lock their bones
In the dumb piles of Chested brasse, and stones.
Th'art rich in thy own fame, and needest not
These *Marble-frailties*, nor the *gilded blot*
Of posthume honours; There is not one sand
Sleeps o'r thy grave, but can outbid that hand
And pencill too, so that of force wee must
Confesse their *heaps* shew lesser than thy *dust*.

   And (blessed soule!) though this my sorrow can
Adde nought to thy perfections, yet as man
Subject to Envy, and the common fate
It may redeem thee to a fairer date;
As some blind Dial, when the day is done,
Can tell us at mid-night, *There was a Sun*,
So these perhaps, though much beneath thy fame,
May keep some weak remembrance of thy name,
And to the faith of better times Commend
Thy loyall upright life, and gallant End.

> *Nomen & arma locum servant, te, amice, nequivi*
> *Conspicere*, ——

Upon a Cloke lent him by Mr. *J. Ridsley*

Here, take again thy *Sack-cloth*! and thank heav'n
Thy Courtship hath not kill'd me; Is't not Even
Whether wee dye by peecemeale, or at once
Since both but ruine, why then for the nonce
Didst husband my afflictions, and cast o're
Me this forc'd *Hurdle* to inflame the score?
Had I neer *London* in this *Rug* been seen
Without doubt I had executed been
For some bold *Irish* spy, and crosse a sledge
Had layn mess'd up for their *foure gates* and *bridge.*
When first I bore it, my oppressed feet
Would needs perswade me, 'twas some *Leaden sheet*;
Such deep Impressions, and such dangerous holes
Were made, that I began to doubt my soals,
And ev'ry step (so neer necessity)
Devoutly wish'd some honest Cobler by,
Besides it was so short, the *Jewish rag*
Seem'd Circumcis'd, but had a *Gentile* shag.
Hadst thou been with me on that day, when wee
Left craggie *Biston*, and the fatall *Dee*
When beaten with fresh storms, and late mishap
It shar'd the office of a *Cloke*, and *Cap*,
To see how 'bout my clouded head it stood
Like a thick *Turband*, or some Lawyers *Hood*,
While the stiffe, hollow pletes on ev'ry side
Like *Conduit-pipes* rain'd from the *Bearded hide*,
I know thou wouldst in spite of that day's fate
Let loose thy mirth at my new shape and state,
And with a shallow smile or two professe
Some *Sarazin* had lost the *Clowted Dresse.*
Didst ever see the *good wife* (as they say)
March in her short cloke on the *Christning* day,
With what soft motions she salutes the Church,
And leaves the Bedrid Mother in the lurch;

Just so Jogg'd I, while my dull horse did trudge
Like a Circuit-beast plagu'd with a goutie Judge.
    But this was Civill. I have since known more
And worser pranks: One night (as heretofore
Th' hast known) for want of change (a thing which I
And *Bias* us'd before me) I did lye
Pure *Adamite*, and simply for that end
Resolv'd, and made this for my bosome-*friend*.
O that thou hadst been there next morn, that I
Might teach thee new *Micro-cosmo-graphie*!
Thou wouldst have ta'ne me, as I naked stood,
For one of th' *seven pillars* before the floud,
Such *Characters* and *Hierogliphicks* were
In one night worn, that thou mightst justly swear
I'd slept in *Cere-cloth*, or at *Bedlam* where
The mad men lodge in straw, I'le not forbear
To tell thee all, his wild *Impress* and *tricks*
Like *Speeds* old *Britans* made me look, or *Picts*;
His villainous, biting, *Wire-embraces*
Had seal'd in me more strange formes and faces
Than *Children* see in dreams, or thou has read
In *Arras, Puppet-playes*, and *Ginger-bread,*
With *angled Schemes*, and *Crosses* that bred fear
Of being handled by some *Conjurer*,
And neerer thou wouldst think (such *strokes* were drawn)
I'd been some rough statue of *Fetter-lane*,
Nay, I believe, had I that instant been
By *Surgeons* or *Apothecaries* seen,
They had Condemned my raz'd skin to be
Some walking *Herball*, or *Anatomie*.
    But (thanks to th'day!) 'tis off. I'd now advise
Thee friend to put this peece to Merchandize;
The *Pedlars* of our age have business yet,
And gladly would against the *Fayr-day* fit
Themselves with such a *Roofe*, that can secure
Their *Wares* from *Dogs* and *Cats* rain'd in showre,

It shall performe; or if this will not doe
'Twill take the *Ale-wives* sure; 'Twill make them *two*
Fine Roomes of *One*, and spread upon a stick
Is a partition without Lime or Brick.
Horn'd obstinacie! how my heart doth fret
To think what *Mouthes* and *Elbowes* it would set
In a wet day? have you for two pence e're
Seen King *Harryes* Chappell at *Westminster*,
Where in their dustie gowns of *Brasse* and *Stone*
The Judges lye, and markt you how each one
In sturdie Marble-plets about the knee
Bears up to shew his legs and symmetrie?
Just so would this; That I think't weav'd upon
Some stiffneckt *Brownists* exercising loome.
O that thou hadst it when this Jugling fate
Of Souldierie first seiz'd me! at what rate
Would I have bought it then, what was there but
I would have giv'n for the *Compendious hutt*?
I doe not doubt but (if the weight could please,)
'Twould guard me better than a *Lapland-lease*,
Or a *German* shirt with Inchanted lint
Stuff'd through, and th'devils *beard* and *face* weav'd in't.
    But I have done. And think not, friend, that I
This freedome took to Jeere thy Courtesie,
I thank thee for't, and I believe my Muse
So known to thee, thou'lt not suspect abuse;
She did this, 'cause (perhaps) thy *love* paid thus
Might with my *thanks* out-live thy *Cloke*, and *Us*.

An Elegie on the death of Mr. *R. Hall*, slain at *Pontefract*, 1648

I knew it would be thus! And my Just fears
Of thy great spirit are Improv'd to tears.
Yet flow these not from any base distrust
Of a fair name, or that thy honour must
Confin'd to those cold reliques sadly sit
In the same Cell an obscure Anchorite.
Such low distempers *Murther*, they that must
Abuse thee so, *weep* not, but *wound* thy dust.
 But I past such dimme Mourners can descrie
Thy fame above all Clouds of obloquie,
And like the Sun with his victorious rayes
Charge through that darkness to the last of dayes.
'Tis true, fair *Manhood* hath a *female* Eye,
And tears are beauteous in a Victorie,
Nor are wee so high-proofe, but griefe will find
Through all our guards a way to wound the mind;
But in thy fall what addes the brackish summe
More than a blott unto thy *Martyrdome*,
Which scorns such wretched suffrages, and stands
More by thy single worth, than our whole bands.
Yet could the puling tribute rescue ought
In this sad losse, or wert thou to be brought
Back here by tears, I would in any wise
Pay down the summe, or quite Consume my Eyes.
Thou fell'st our double ruine, and this rent
Forc'd in thy life shak'd both the *Church and tent*,
Learning in others steales them from the *Van*,
And basely wise *Emasculates* the man,
But lodged in thy brave soul the *bookish feat*
Serve'd only as the light unto thy *heat*;
Thus when some quitted action, to their shame,
And only got a *discreet Cowards* name,
Thou with thy bloud mad'st purchase of renown,

And diedst the glory of the *Sword* and *Gown*,
Thy bloud hath hallow'd *Pomfret*, and this blow
(Prophan'd before) hath Church'd the Castle now.
    Nor is't a Common valour we deplore,
But such as with *fifteen* a *hundred* bore,
And lightning like (not coopt within a wall)
In stormes of *fire* and *steele* fell on them all.
Thou wert no *Wool-sack* souldier, nor of those
Whose Courage lies in *winking* at their foes,
That live at *loop holes*, and consume their breath
On *Match* or *Pipes*, and sometimes *peepe* at death;
No, it were sinne to number these with thee,
But that (thus poiz'd) our losse wee better see.
The fair and open valour was thy *shield*,
And thy known station, the *defying field*.
    Yet these in thee I would not *Vertues* call,
But that this age must know, that thou hadst all.
Those richer graces that adorn'd thy mind
Like stars of the *first magnitude*, so shin'd,
That if oppos'd unto these lesser lights
All we can say, is this, *They were fair nights*.
Thy *Piety* and *Learning* did unite,
And though with *Sev'rall beames* made up *one light*,
And such thy Judgement was, that I dare swear
Whole *Counsels* might as soon, and *Synods* erre.
    But all these now are out! and as some *Star*
Hurl'd in Diurnall motions from far,
And seen to droop at night, is vainly sed
To fall, and find an *Occidentall bed*,
Though in that other world what wee Judge *West*
Proves *Elevation*, and a new, fresh *East*.
So though our weaker sense denies us sight
And bodies cannot trace the *Spirits* flight,
Wee know those graces to be still in thee,
But wing'd above us to eternitie.
Since then (thus flown) thou art so much refin'd,

That we can only reach thee with the mind,
  I will not in this *dark* and *narrow glasse*
Let thy scant *shadow*, for *Perfections* passe,
But leave thee to be read more high, more queint,
In thy own bloud a *Souldier* and a *Saint*.

  —— *Salve æternum mihi maxime Palla!*
  Æternumque vale! ——

To my worthy friend Master *T. Lewes*

Sees not my friend, what a deep snow
Candies our Countries wooddy brow?
The yeelding branch his load scarse bears
Opprest with snow, and *frozen tears*,
While the *dumb* rivers slowly float,
All bound up in an *Icie Coat*.
    Let us meet then! and while this world
In wild *Excentricks* now is hurld,
Keep wee, like nature, the same *Key*,
And walk in our forefathers way;
Why any more cast wee an Eye
On what *may come*, not what is *nigh*?
Why vex our selves with *feare*, or *hope*
And cares beyond our *Horoscope*?
Who into future times would peere
Looks oft beyond his terme set here,
And cannot goe into those grounds
But through a *Church-yard* which them bounds;
Sorrows and sighes and searches spend
And draw our bottome to an end,
But discreet Joyes lengthen the lease
Without which life were a disease,
And who this age a Mourner goes,
Doth with his tears but feed his foes.

From *Silex Scintillans I*

The Authors
PREFACE
To the following
HYMNS.

That this Kingdom hath abounded with those ingenious persons, which in the late notion are termed *Wits*, is too well known. Many of them having cast away all their fair portion of time, in no better imployments, then a deliberate search, or excogitation of *idle words*, and a most vain, insatiable desire to be reputed *Poets*; leaving behinde them no other Monuments of those excellent abilities conferred upon them, but such as they may (with a *Predecessor* of theirs) term *Parricides*, and a soul-killing Issue; for that is the Βραβεῖου, and Laureate *Crown*, which idle *Poems* will certainly bring to their unrelenting Authors.

And well it were for them, if those willingly-studied and wilfully-published vanities could defile no *spirits*, but their own; but the *case* is far worse. These *Vipers* survive their *Parents*, and for many ages after (like *Epidemic* diseases) infect whole Generations, corrupting always and unhallowing the best-gifted *Souls*, and the most capable *Vessels*: for whose sanctification and well-fare, the glorious *Son* of God laid down his *life*, and suffered the pretious *blood* of his blessed and innocent *heart* to be poured out. In the mean time it cannot be denied, but these men are had in remembrance, though we cannot say with any comfort, *Their memorial is blessed*; for, that I may speak no more then the truth (let their passionate *worshippers* say what they please) all the commendations that can be justly given them, will amount to no more, then what *Prudentius* the Christian-sacred *Poet* bestowed upon *Symmachus*;

Os dignum aeterno tinctum quod fulgeat auro
Si mallet laudare deum: cui sordida monstra
Prætulit, & liquidam temeravit crimine vocem;
Haud aliter, quàm cum rastris qui tentat eburnis
Cænosum versare solum, &c. ———

In English thus,

A wit most worthy in tryed Gold to shine,
Immortal Gold! had he sung the divine
Praise of his Maker: to whom he preferr'd
Obscene, vile fancies, and prophanely marr'd
A rich, rare stile with sinful, lewd contents;
No otherwise, then if with Instruments
Of polish'd Ivory, some drudge should stir
A dirty sink, &c. ———

This *comparison* is nothing odious, and it is as *true*, as it is *apposite*;
for a *good* wit in a *bad* subject, is (as *Solomon* said of the *fair* and *foolish
woman*) *Like a jewel of gold in a swines snowt*, Prov. 11.22. Nay, the more
acute the *Author is*, there is so much the more danger and death in the
work. Where the *Sun* is busie upon a *dung-hill*, the *issue* is always some
unclean *vermine*. Divers persons of eminent piety and learning (I
meddle not with the seditious and *Schismatical*) have, long before
my time, taken notice of this *malady*; for the complaint against *vitious
verse*, even by peaceful and obedient *spirits*, is of some antiquity in
this Kingdom. And yet, as if the evil consequence attending this
inveterate *error*, were but a small thing, there is sprung very lately
another prosperous *device* to assist it in the subversion of *souls*. Those
that want the *Genius* of *verse*, fall to *translating*; and the people are
(every *term*) plentifully furnished with various *Foraign vanities*; so
that the most lascivious compositions of *France* and *Italy* are here
naturalized and made *English*: And this (as it is sadly observed) with
so much favor and success, that nothing *takes* (as they rightly phrase
it) like a *Romance*. And very frequently (if that *Character* be not an
Ivy-bush) the *buyer* receives this lewd ware from *persons of honor*:
who want not reason to forbear, much private misfortune having

sprung from no other *seed* at first, then some infectious and dissolving *Legend*.

To continue (after years of discretion) in this *vanity*, is an inexcusable desertion of *pious sobriety*: and to persist so to the end, is a wilful despising of Gods *sacred exhortations*, by a constant, sensual volutation or wallowing in *impure thoughts* and *scurrilous conceits*, which both defile their Authors, and as many more, as they are communicated to. If *every idle word shall be accounted for*, and if *no corrupt communication should proceed out of our mouths*, how desperate (I beseech you) is their condition, who all their life time, and out of meer design, study *lascivious fictions*: then carefully record and publish them, that instead of *grace* and *life*, they *may minister sin and death* unto their readers? It was wisely considered, and piously said by one, *That he would read no idle books; both in regard of love to his own soul, and pity unto his that made them, for* (said he) *if I be corrupted by them, their Composer is immediatly a cause of my ill: and at the day of reckoning (though now dead) must give an account for it, because I am corrupted by his bad example, which he left behinde him: I will write none, lest I hurt them that come after me: I will read none, lest I augment his punishment that is gone before me. I will neither write, nor read, lest I prove a foe to my own soul: while I live, I sin too much; let me not continue longer in wickedness, then I do in life.* It is a sentence of sacred authority, that *he that is dead, is freed from sin*; because he cannot in that state, which is without the *body*, sin any more; but he *that writes idle books*, makes for himself another *body*, in which he always *lives*, and sins (after *death*) as *fast* and as *foul*, as ever he did in his *life*; which very consideration, deserves to be a sufficient *Antidote* against this evil disease.

And here, because I would prevent a just *censure* by my free *confession*, I must remember, that I my self have for many years together, languished of this very *sickness*; and it is no long time since I have recovered. But (blessed be God for it!) I have by his saving assistance supprest my *greatest follies*, and those which escaped from me, are (I think) as innoxious, as most of that *vein* use to be; besides, they are interlined with many virtuous, and some pious mixtures. What I speak of them, is truth; but let no man mistake it for an *extenuation* of faults, as if I intended an *Apology* for *them*, or my *self*, who am conscious of so much *guilt* in *both*, as can never be expiated without *special sorrows*, and that cleansing and pretious *effusion* of my Almighty Redeemer: and if the world will be so charitable, as to grant my request, I do here most humbly and earnestly beg that none would read them.

But an idle or sensual *subject* is not all the *poyson* in these Pamphlets. Certain Authors have been so irreverendly bold, as to dash *Scriptures*, and the *sacred Relatives* of God with their impious conceits. And (which I cannot speak without grief of heart) some of those desperate *adventurers* may (I think) be reckoned amongst the principal or most learned Writers of *English verse*.

Others of a later *date*, being corrupted (it may be) by that evil *Genius*, which came in with the publique distractions, have stuffed their books with *Oathes, horrid Execrations*, and a most gross and studied *filthiness*. But the *hurt* that ensues by the publication of *pieces* so notoriously ill, lies heavily upon the *Stationers* account, who ought in conscience to refuse them, when they are put into his hands. No *loss* is so doleful as that *gain*, that will endamage the soul; he that *prints* lewdness and impieties, is that mad man in the *Proverbs*, who *casteth firebrands, arrows and death*.

The suppression of this pleasing and prevailing *evil*, lies not altogether in the power of the *Magistrate*; for it will flie abroad in *Manuscripts*, when it fails of entertainment at the *press*. The true remedy lies wholly in their bosoms, who are the gifted persons, by a wise exchange of *vain* and *vitious subjects*, for *divine Themes* and *Celestial praise*. The *performance* is easie, and were it the most difficult in the world, the *reward* is so glorious, that it infinitely transcends it: for *they that turn many to righteousness, shall shine like the stars for ever and ever.* whence follows this undenyable *inference*, That the *corrupting of many*, being a contrary work, the *recompense* must be so too; and then I know nothing reserved for them, but *the blackness of darkness for ever*, from which (O God!) deliver all penitent and reformed *Spirits!*

The first, that with any effectual success attempted a *diversion* of this foul and overflowing *stream*, was the blessed man, Mr. *George Herbert*, whose holy *life* and *verse* gained many pious *Converts*, (of

whom I am the least) and gave the first check to a most flourishing
and admired *wit* of his time. After him followed diverse, – *Sed non
passibus aequis*; they had more of *fashion*, then *force*: And the *reason* of
their so vast *distance* from him, besides differing *spirits* and *qualifica-
tions* (for his *measure* was eminent) I suspect to be, because they
aimed more at *verse*, then *perfection*; as may be easily gathered by
their frequent *impressions*, and numerous pages: Hence sprang those
wide, those weak, and lean *conceptions*, which in the most inclinable
Reader will scarce give any nourishment or help to *devotion*; for not
flowing from a true, practick piety, it was impossible they should
effect those things abroad, which they never had acquaintance with
at home; being onely the productions of a common spirit, and the
obvious ebullitions of that light humor, which takes the pen in hand,
out of no other consideration, then to be seen in print. It is true
indeed, that to give up our thoughts to pious *Themes* and *Contempla-
tions* (if it be done for pieties sake) is a great *step* towards *perfection*;
because it will *refine*, and *dispose* to devotion and sanctity. And
further, it will *procure* for us (so easily communicable is that *loving
spirit*) some small *prelibation* of those heavenly *refreshments*, which
descend but seldom, and then very sparingly, upon *men* of an ordin-
ary or indifferent *holyness*: but he that desires to excel in this kinde of
Hagiography, or holy writing, must strive (by all means) for *perfection*
and true *holyness*, that a *door may be opened to him in heaven*, Rev. 4.1.
and then he will he able to write (with *Hierotheus* and holy *Herbert*) A
true Hymn.

To effect this in some measure, I have begged leave to communi-
cate this my poor *Talent* to the *Church*, under the *protection* and *conduct*
of her *glorious Head*: who (if he will vouchsafe to *own* it, and *go along*
with it) can make it as useful now in the *publick*, as it hath been to me
in *private*. In the *perusal* of it, you will (peradventure) observe some
passages, whose *history* or *reason* may seem something *remote*; but were
they brought *nearer*, and plainly exposed to your view, (though that
(perhaps) might quiet your *curiosity*) yet would it not conduce much
to your greater *advantage*. And therefore I must desire you to accept
of them in that *latitude*, which is already alowed them. By the last
Poems in the book (were not that *mistake* here prevented) you

would judge all to be *fatherless*, and the *Edition* posthume; for (indeed) *I was nigh unto death*, and am still at no great distance from it; which was the necessary reason for that solemn and accomplished *dress*, you will now finde this *impression* in.

But *the God of the spirits of all flesh*, hath granted me a further use of *mine*, then I did look for in the *body*; and when I expected, and had (by his assistance) prepared for a *message* of *death*, then did he *answer* me with *life*; I hope to his *glory*, and my great *advantage*: that I may flourish not with *leafe* onely, but with some *fruit* also; which *hope* and earnest *desire* of his poor *Creature*, I humbly beseech him to perfect and fulfil for his dear *Sons* sake, unto *whom*, with *him* and the most holy and loving *Spirit*, be ascribed by *Angels*, by *Men*, and by all his *Works*, All Glory, and Wisdom, and Dominion, in this the *temporal* and in the *Eternal* Being. *Amen.*

Newton by Usk, near
Sketh-rock, Septemb. 30
1654.

Regeneration

A Ward, and still in bonds, one day
   I stole abroad,
It was high-spring, and all the way
   Primrose'd, and hung with shade;
  Yet, was it frost within,
    And surly winds
Blasted my infant buds, and sinne
   Like Clouds ecclips'd my mind.

2

Storm'd thus; I straight perceiv'd my spring
   Meere stage, and show,
My walke a monstrous, mountain'd thing
   Rough-cast with Rocks, and snow;
  And as a Pilgrims Eye
    Far from reliefe,
Measures the melancholy skye
   Then drops, and rains for griefe,

3

So sigh'd I upwards still, at last
   'Twixt steps, and falls
I reach'd the pinacle, where plac'd
   I found a paire of scales,
  I tooke them up and layd
    In th'one late paines,
The other smoake, and pleasures weigh'd
   But prov'd the heavier graines;

4

With that, some cryed, *Away*; straight I
   Obey'd, and led
Full East, a faire, fresh field could spy
   Some call'd it, *Jacobs Bed*;

A Virgin-soile, which no
   Rude feet ere trod,
Where (since he stept there,) only go
   Prophets, and friends of God.

    5

Here, I repos'd; but scarse well set,
   A grove descryed
Of stately height, whose branches met
   And mixt on every side;
   I entred, and once in
    (Amaz'd to see't,)
Found all was chang'd, and a new spring
   Did all my senses greet;

    6

The unthrift Sunne shot vitall gold
   A thousand peeces,
And heaven its azure did unfold
   Checqur'd with snowie fleeces,
   The aire was all in spice
    And every bush
A garland wore; Thus fed my Eyes
   But all the Eare lay hush.

    7

Only a little Fountain lent
   Some use for Eares,
And on the dumbe shades language spent
   The Musick of her teares;
   I drew her neere, and found
    The Cisterne full
Of divers stones, some bright, and round
   Others ill-shap'd, and dull.

8

The first (pray marke,) as quick as light
                    Danc'd through the floud,
But, th'last more heavy then the night
                    Nail'd to the Center stood;
          I wonder'd much, but tyr'd
                    At last with thought,
My restless Eye that still desir'd
                    As strange an object brought;

9

It was a banke of flowers, where I descried
                    (Though 'twas mid-day,)
Some fast asleepe, others broad-eyed
                    And taking in the Ray,
          Here musing long, I heard
                    A rushing wind
Which still increas'd, but whence it stirr'd
                    No where I could not find;

10

I turn'd me round, and to each shade
                    Dispatch'd an Eye,
To sec, if any leafe had made
                    Least motion, or Reply,
          But while I listning sought
                    My mind to ease
By knowing, where 'twas, or where not,
                    It whisper'd; *Where I please.*

Lord, then said I, *On me one breath,*
And let me dye before my death!

Song of Songs 5.17
Arise O North, and come thou South-wind, and blow upon my
garden, that the spices thereof may flow out.

Resurrection and Immortality

Hebrews 10.20

By that new, and living way, which he hath prepared for us, through the veile,
which is his flesh.

Body

1

Oft have I seen, when that renewing breath
   That binds, and loosens death
Inspir'd a quickning power through the dead
    Creatures a bed,
  Some drowsie silk-worme creepe
    From that long sleepe
And in weake, infant hummings chime, and knell
   About her silent Cell
Untill at last full with the vitall Ray
    She wing'd away,
  And proud with life, and sence,
    Heav'ns rich Expence,
Esteem'd (vaine things!) of two whole Elements
   As meane, and span-extents.
Shall I then thinke such providence will be
    Lesse friend to me?
  Or that he can endure to be unjust
Who keeps his Covenant even with our dust.

Soule

2

Poore, querulous handfull! was't for this
   I taught thee all that is?
Unbowel'd nature, shew'd thee her recruits,
    And Change of suits
  And how of death we make
    A meere mistake,

For no thing can to *Nothing* fall, but still
   Incorporates by skill,
And then returns, and from the wombe of things
    Such treasure brings
   As *Phenix*-like renew'th
    Both life, and youth;
For a preserving spirit doth still passe
   Untainted through this Masse,
Which doth resolve, produce, and ripen all
    That to it fall;
   Nor are those births which we
    Thus suffering see
Destroy'd at all; But when times restles wave
    Their substance doth deprave
And the more noble *Essence* finds his house
    Sickly, and loose,
   He, ever young, doth wing
    Unto that spring,
And *source* of spirits, where he takes his lot
   Till time no more shall rot
His passive Cottage; which (though laid aside,)
    Like some spruce Bride,
Shall one day rise, and cloath'd with shining light
    All pure, and bright
   Re-marry to the soule, for 'tis most plaine
   Thou only fal'st to be refin'd againe.

3

Then I that here saw darkly in a glasse
    But mists, and shadows passe,
And, by their owne weake *Shine*, did search the springs
    And Course of things
   Shall with Inlightned Rayes
    Peirce all their wayes;
And as thou saw'st, I in a thought could goe
   To heav'n, or Earth below

To reade some *Starre*, or *Min'rall*, and in State
                    There often sate,
            So shalt thou then with me
                    (Both wing'd, and free,)
Rove in that mighty, and eternall light
            Where no rude shade, or night
Shall dare approach us; we shall there no more
                    Watch stars, or pore
            Through melancholly clouds, and say
                    Would it were Day!
            One everlasting *Saboth* there shall runne
            Without *Succession*, and without a *Sunne*.

Daniel 12.13
But goe thou thy way untill the end be, for thou shalt rest, and
stand up in thy lot, at the end of the dayes.

Religion

My God, when I walke in those groves,
And leaves thy spirit doth still fan,
I see in each shade that there growes
An Angell talking with a man.

Under a *Juniper*, some house,
Or the coole *Mirtles* canopie,
Others beneath an *Oakes* greene boughs,
Or at some *fountaines* bubling Eye;

Here *Jacob* dreames, and wrestles; there
Elias by a Raven is fed,
Another time by th' Angell, where
He brings him water with his bread;

In *Abr'hams* Tent the winged guests
(O how familiar then was heaven!)
Eate, drinke, discourse, sit downe, and rest
Untill the Coole, and shady *Even*;

Nay thou thy selfe, my God, in *fire*,
Whirle-winds, and *Clouds*, and the *soft voice*
Speak'st there so much, that I admire
We have no Conf'rence in these daies;

Is the truce broke? or 'cause we have
A mediatour now with thee,
Doest thou therefore old Treaties wave
And by appeales from him decree?

Or is't so, as some green heads say
That now all miracles must cease?
Though thou hast promis'd they should stay
The tokens of the Church, and peace;

No, no; Religion is a Spring
That from some secret, golden Mine

Derives her birth, and thence doth bring
Cordials in every drop, and Wine;

But in her long, and hidden Course
Passing through the Earths darke veines,
Growes still from better unto worse,
And both her taste, and colour staines,

Then drilling on, learnes to encrease
False *Ecchoes*, and Confused sounds,
And unawares doth often seize
On veines of *Sulphur* under ground;

So poison'd, breaks forth in some Clime,
And at first sight doth many please,
But drunk, is puddle, or meere slime
And 'stead of Phisick, a disease;

Just such a tainted sink we have
Like that *Samaritans* dead *Well*,
Nor must we for the Kernell crave
Because most voices like the *shell*.

Heale then these waters, Lord; or bring thy flock,
Since these are troubled, to the springing rock,
Looke downe great Master of the feast; O shine,
And turn once more our *Water* into *Wine*!

Song of Songs 4.12
*My sister, my spouse is as a garden Inclosed, as a Spring shut
up, and a fountain sealed up.*

The Search

'Tis now cleare day: I see a Rose
Bud in the bright East, and disclose
The Pilgrim-Sunne; all night have I
Spent in a roving Extasie
To find my Saviour; I have been
As far as *Bethlem*, and have seen
His Inne, and Cradle; Being there
I met the *Wise-men*, askt them where
He might be found, or what starre can
Now point him out, grown up a Man?
To *Egypt* hence I fled, ran o're
All her parcht bosome to *Nile's* shore
Her yearly nurse; came back, enquir'd
Amongst the *Doctors*, and desir'd
To see the *Temple*, but was shown
A little dust, and for the Town
A heap of ashes, where some sed
A small bright sparkle was a bed,
Which would one day (beneath the pole,)
Awake, and then refine the whole.
    Tyr'd here, I come to *Sychar*; thence
To *Jacobs wel*, bequeathed since
Unto his sonnes, (where often they
In those calme, golden Evenings lay
Watring their flocks, and having spent
Those white dayes, drove home to the Tent
Their *well-fleec'd* traine;) And here (O fate!)
I sit, where once my Saviour sate;
The angry Spring in bubbles swell'd
Which broke in sighes still, as they fill'd,
And whisper'd, *Jesus had been there*
But *Jacobs children would not heare.*
Loath hence to part, at last I rise
But with the fountain in my Eyes,

And here a fresh search is decreed
He must be found, where he did bleed;
I walke the garden, and there see
Idæa's of his Agonie,
And moving anguishments that set
His blest face in a bloudy sweat;
I climb'd the Hill, perus'd the Crosse
Hung with my gaine, and his great losse,
Never did tree beare fruit like this,
Balsam of Soules, the bodyes blisse;
But, O his grave! where I saw lent
(For he had none,) a Monument,
An undefil'd, and new-heaw'd one,
But there was not the *Corner-stone*;
Sure (then said I,) my Quest is vaine,
Hee'le not be found, where he was slaine,
So mild a Lamb can never be
'Midst so much bloud, and Crueltie;
I'le to the Wildernesse, and can
Find beasts more mercifull then man,
He liv'd there safe, 'twas his retreat
From the fierce *Jew*, and *Herods* heat,
And forty dayes withstood the fell,
And high temptations of hell;
With Seraphins there talked he
His fathers flaming ministrie,
He heav'nd their *walks*, and with his eyes
Made those wild shades a Paradise,
Thus was the desert sanctified
To be the refuge of his bride;
I'le thither then; see, It is day,
The Sun's broke through to guide my way.
    But as I urg'd thus, and writ down
What pleasures should my Journey crown,
What silent paths, what shades, and Cells,
Faire, virgin-flowers, and hallow'd *Wells*

I should rove in, and rest my head
Where my deare Lord did often tread,
Sugring all dangers with successe,
Me thought I heard one singing thus;

1

Leave, leave, thy gadding thoughts;
Who Pores
and spies
Still out of Doores
descries
Within them nought.

2

The skinne, and shell of things
Though faire,
are not
Thy wish, nor pray'r
but got
By meer Despair
of wings.

3

To rack old Elements,
or Dust
and say
Sure here he must
needs stay
Is not the way,
nor just.
Search well another world; who studies this,
Travels in Clouds, seeks *Manna*, where none is.

Acts 17.27–28

That they should seek the Lord, if happily they might feel after him,
and finde him, though he be not far off from every one of us, for in
him we live, and move, and have our being.

Isaacs Marriage

Genesis 24.63

And Isaac *went out to pray in the field at the Even-tide, and he lift up his eyes, and saw, and behold, the Camels were coming.*

Praying! and to be married? It was rare,
But now 'tis monstrous; and that pious care
Though of our selves, is so much out of date,
That to renew't were to degenerate.
But thou a Chosen sacrifice wert given,
And offer'd up so early unto heaven
Thy flames could not be out; Religion was
Ray'd into thee, like beams into a glass,
Where, as thou grewst, it multipli'd and shin'd
The sacred Constellation of thy mind.
But being for a bride, prayer was such
A decryed course, sure it prevail'd not much.
Had'st ne'r an oath, nor Complement? thou wert
An odde dull sutor; Hadst thou but the art
Of these our dayes, thou couldst have coyn'd thee twenty
New sev'ral oathes, and Complements (too) plenty;
O sad, and wilde excesse! and happy those
White dayes, that durst no impious mirth expose!
When Conscience by lew'd use had not lost sense,
Nor bold-fac'd custome banish'd Innocence;
Thou hadst no pompous train, nor *Antick* crowd
Of young, gay swearers, with their needlesse, lowd
Retinue; All was here smooth as thy bride
And calm like her, or that mild Evening-tide;
Yet, hadst thou nobler guests: Angels did wind
And rove about thee, guardians of thy minde,
These fetch'd thee home thy bride, and all the way
Advis'd thy servant what to do, and say;
These taught him at the *well*, and thither brought
The Chast, and lovely object of thy thought;

But here was ne'r a Complement, not one
Spruce, supple cringe, or study'd look put on,
All was plain, modest truth: Nor did she come
In *rowles* and *Curles*, mincing and stately dumb,
But in a Virgins native blush and fears
Fresh as those roses, which the day-spring wears.
O sweet, divine simplicity! O grace
Beyond a Curled lock, or painted face!
A *Pitcher* too she had, nor thought it much
To carry that, which some would scorn to touch;
With which in mild, chast language she did wooe
To draw him drink, and for his Camels too.
   And now thou knewest her coming, It was time
To get thee wings on, and devoutly climbe
Unto thy God, for Marriage of all states
Makes most unhappy, or most fortunates;
This brought thee forth, where now thou didst undress
Thy soul, and with new pinions refresh
Her wearied wings, which so restor'd did flye
Above the stars, a track unknown, and high,
And in her piercing flight perfum'd the ayer
Scatt'ring the *Myrrhe*, and incense of thy pray'r.
So from *Lahai-roi's* Well some spicie cloud
Woo'd by the Sun swels up to be his shrowd,
And from his moist wombe weeps a fragrant showre,
Which, scatter'd in a thousand pearls, each flowre
And herb partakes, where having stood awhile
And something coold the parch'd, and thirstie Isle,
The thankful Earth unlocks her self, and blends,
A thousand odours, which (all mixt,) she sends
Up in one cloud, and so returns the skies
That dew they lent, a breathing sacrifice.
   Thus soar'd thy soul, who (though young,) didst inherit
Together with his bloud, thy fathers spirit,
Whose active zeal, and tried faith were to thee
Familiar ever since thy Infancie.

Others were tym'd, and train'd up to't but thou
Diddst thy swift yeers in piety out-grow,
Age made them rev'rend, and a snowie head,
But thou wert so, e're time his snow could shed;
Then, who would truly limne thee out, must paint
First, *a young Patriarch*, then a *marri'd Saint*.

The Showre

'Twas so, I saw thy birth: That drowsie Lake
From her faint bosome breath'd thee, the disease
Of her sick waters, and Infectious Ease.
   But, now at Even
   Too grosse for heaven,
Thou fall'st in teares, and weep'st for thy mistake.

2

Ah! it is so with me; oft have I prest
Heaven with a lazie breath, but fruitles this
Peirc'd not; Love only can with quick accesse
   Unlock the way,
   When all else stray
The smoke, and Exhalations of the brest.

3

Yet, if as thou doest melt, and with thy traine
Of drops make soft the Earth, my eyes could weep
O're my hard heart, that's bound up, and asleep,
   Perhaps at last
   (Some such showres past,)
My God would give a Sun-shine after raine.

Distraction

O knit me, that am crumbled dust! the heape
            Is all dispers'd, and cheape;
        Give for a handfull, but a thought
            And it is bought;
                Hadst thou
Made me a starre, a pearle, or a rain-bow,
            The beames I then had shot
            My light had lessend not,
                But now
I find my selfe the lesse, the more I grow;
                The world
Is full of voices; Man is call'd, and hurl'd
            By each, he answers all,
            Knows ev'ry note, and call,
                Hence, still
Fresh dotage tempts, or old usurps his will.
Yet, hadst thou clipt my wings, when Coffin'd in
            This quicken'd masse of sinne,
        And saved that light, which freely thou
            Didst then bestow,
                I feare
I should have spurn'd, and said thou didst forbeare;
            Or that thy store was lesse,
            But now since thou didst blesse
                So much,
I grieve, my God! that thou hast made me such.
                I grieve?
O, yes! thou know'st I doe; Come, and releive
        And tame, and keepe downe with thy light
        Dust that would rise, and dimme my sight,
            Lest left alone too long
            Amidst the noise, and throng,
                Oppressed I
Striving to save the whole, by parcells dye.

The Pursuite

Lord! what a busie, restles thing
      Hast thou made man?
Each day, and houre he is on wing,
      Rests not a span;
Then having lost the Sunne, and light
      By clouds surpriz'd
He keepes a Commerce in the night
      With aire disguis'd;
Hadst thou given to this active dust
      A state untir'd,
The lost Sonne had not left the huske
      Nor home desir'd;
That was thy secret, and it is
      Thy mercy too,
For when all failes to bring to blisse,
      Then, this must doe.
Ah! Lord! and what a Purchase will that be
To take us sick, that sound would not take thee?

¶

Thou that know'st for whom I mourne,
 And why these teares appeare,
That keep'st account, till he returne
 Of all his dust left here;
As easily thou mightst prevent
 As now produce these teares,
And adde unto that day he went
 A faire supply of yeares.
But 'twas my sinne that forc'd thy hand
 To cull this *Prim-rose* out,
That by thy early choice forewarn'd
 My soule might looke about.
O what a vanity is man!
 How like the Eyes quick winke
His Cottage failes; whose narrow span
 Begins even at the brink!
Nine months thy hands are fashioning us,
 And many yeares (alas!)
E're we can lisp, or ought discusse
 Concerning thee, must passe;
Yet have I knowne thy slightest things
 A *feather*, or a *shell*,
A *stick*, or *Rod* which some Chance brings
 The best of us excell,
Yea, I have knowne these shreds out last
 A faire-compacted frame
And for one *Twenty* we have past
 Almost outlive our name.
Thus hast thou plac'd in mans outside
 Death to the Common Eye,
That heaven within him might abide,
 And close eternitie;
Hence, youth, and folly (mans first shame,)
 Are put unto the slaughter,

And serious thoughts begin to tame
    The wise-mans-madnes *Laughter*;
Dull, wretched wormes! that would not keepe
    Within our first faire bed,
But out of *Paradise* must creepe
    For ev'ry foote to tread;
Yet, had our Pilgrimage bin free,
    And smooth without a thorne,
Pleasures had foil'd Eternitie,
    And *tares* had choakt the *Corne*.
Thus by the Crosse Salvation runnes,
    Affliction is a mother,
Whose painfull throws yield many sons,
    Each fairer than the other;
A silent teare can peirce thy throne,
    When lowd Joyes want a wing,
And sweeter aires streame from a grone,
    Than any arted string;
Thus, Lord, I see my gaine is great,
    My losse but little to it,
Yet something more I must intreate
    And only thou canst doe it.
O let me (like him,) know my End!
    And be as glad to find it,
And whatsoe'r thou shalt Commend,
    Still let thy Servant mind it!
Then make my soule white as his owne,
    My faith as pure, and steddy,
And deck me, Lord, with the same Crowne
    Thou hast crownd him already!

Vanity of Spirit

Quite spent with thoughts I left my Cell, and lay
Where a shrill spring tun'd to the early day.
    I beg'd here long, and gron'd to know
    Who gave the Clouds so brave a bow,
    Who bent the spheres, and circled in
    Corruption with this glorious Ring,
    What is his name, and how I might
    Descry some part of his great light.
I summon'd nature: peirc'd through all her store,
Broke up some seales, which none had touch'd before,
    Her wombe, her bosome, and her head
    Where all her secrets lay a bed
    I rifled quite, and having past
    Through all the Creatures, came at last
    To search my selfe, where I did find
    Traces, and sounds of a strange kind.
Here of this mighty spring, I found some drills,
With Ecchoes beaten from th' eternall hills;
    Weake beames, and fires flash'd to my sight,
    Like a young East, or Moone-shine night,
    Which shew'd me in a nook cast by
    A peece of much antiquity,
    With Hyerogliphicks quite dismembred,
    And broken letters scarce remembred.
I tooke them up, and (much Joy'd,) went about
T' unite those peeces, hoping to find out
    The mystery; but this neer done,
    That little light I had was gone:
    It griev'd me much. At last, said I,
    Since in these veyls my Ecclips'd Eye
    May not approach thee, (for at night
    Who can have commerce with the light?)
    I'le disapparell, and to buy
    But one half glaunce, most gladly dye.

The Retreate

Happy those early dayes! when I
Shin'd in my Angell-infancy.
Before I understood this place
Appointed for my second race,
Or taught my soul to fancy ought
But a white, Celestiall thought,
When yet I had not walkt above
A mile, or two, from my first love,
And looking back (at that short space,)
Could see a glimpse of his bright-face;
When on some *gilded Cloud*, or *flowre*
My gazing soul would dwell an houre,
And in those weaker glories spy
Some shadows of eternity;
Before I taught my tongue to wound
My Conscience with a sinfull sound,
Or had the black art to dispence
A sev'rall sinne to ev'ry sence,
But felt through all this fleshly dresse
Bright *shootes* of everlastingnesse.
   O how I long to travell back
And tread again that ancient track!
That I might once more reach that plaine,
Where first I left my glorious traine,
From whence th' Inlightned spirit sees
That shady City of Palme trees;
But (ah!) my soul with too much stay
Is drunk, and staggers in the way.
Some men a forward motion love,
But I by backward steps would move,
And when this dust falls to the urn
In that state I came return.

¶

Come, come, what doe I here?
            Since he is gone
Each day is grown a dozen year,
            And each houre, one;
            Come, come!
            Cut off the sum,
            By these soil'd teares!
            (Which only thou
            Know'st to be true,)
            Dayes are my feares.

2

Ther's not a wind can stir,
            Or beam passe by,
But strait I think (though far,)
            Thy hand is nigh;
            Come, come!
            Strike these lips dumb:
            This restles breath
            That soiles thy name,
            Will ne'r be tame
            Untill in death.

3

Perhaps some think a tombe
            No house of store,
But a dark, and seal'd up wombe,
            Which ne'r breeds more.
            Come, come!
            Such thoughts benum;
            But I would be
            With him I weep
            A bed, and sleep
            To wake in thee.

¶ Midnight

When to my Eyes
(Whilst deep sleep others catches,)
Thine hoast of spyes
The starres shine in their watches,
I doe survey
Each busie Ray,
And how they work, and wind,
And wish each beame
My soul doth streame,
With the like ardour shin'd;
What Emanations,
Quick vibrations
And bright stirs are there?
What thin Ejections,
Cold Affections,
And slow motions here?

2
Thy heav'ns (some say,)
Are a firie-liquid light,
Which mingling aye
Streames, and flames thus to the sight.
Come then, my god!
Shine on this bloud,
And water in one beame,
And thou shalt see
Kindled by thee
Both liquors burne, and streame.
O what bright quicknes,
Active brightnes,
And celestiall flowes
Will follow after
On that water,
Which thy spirit blowes!

Matthew 3.11

I indeed baptize you with water unto repentance, but he that commeth after me, is mightier than I, whose shooes I am not worthy to beare, he shall baptize you with the holy Ghost, and with fire.

¶

Joy of my life! while left me here,
    And still my Love!
How in thy absence thou dost steere
    Me from above!
    A life well lead
    This truth commends,
    With quick, or dead
    It never ends.

2

Stars are of mighty use: The night
    Is dark, and long;
The Rode foul, and where one goes right,
    Six may go wrong.
    One twinkling ray
    Shot o'r some cloud,
    May clear much way
    And guide a croud.

3

Gods Saints are shining lights: who stays
    Here long must passe
O're dark hills, swift streames, and steep ways
    As smooth as glasse;
    But these all night
    Like Candles, shed
    Their beams, and light
    Us into Bed.

4

They are (indeed,) our Pillar-fires
    Seen as we go,
They are that Cities shining Spires
    We travell too;

A swordlike gleame
Kept man for sin
First *Out*; This beame
Will guide him *In*.

The Morning-watch

O Joyes! Infinite sweetnes! with what flowres,
And shoots of glory, my soul breakes, and buds!
   All the long houres
   Of night, and Rest
   Through the still shrouds
   Of sleep, and Clouds,
  This Dew fell on my Breast;
   O how it *Blouds,*
And *Spirits* all my Earth! heark! In what Rings,
And *Hymning Circulations* the quick world
   Awakes, and sings;
   The rising winds,
   And falling springs,
   Birds, beasts, all things
  Adore him in their kinds.
   Thus all is hurl'd
In sacred *Hymnes*, and *Order*, The great *Chime*
And *Symphony* of nature. Prayer is
   The world in tune,
   A spirit-voyce,
   And vocall joyes
  Whose *Eccho is* heav'ns blisse.
   O let me climbe
When I lye down! The Pious soul by night
Is like a clouded starre, whose beames though sed
   To shed their light
   Under some Cloud
   Yet are above,
   And shine, and move
  Beyond that mistie shrowd.
   So in my Bed
That Curtain'd grave, though sleep, like ashes, hide
My lamp, and life, both shall in thee abide.

¶

Silence, and stealth of dayes! 'tis now
       Since thou art gone,
Twelve hundred houres, and not a brow
       But Clouds hang on.
As he that in some Caves thick damp
       Lockt from the light,
Fixeth a solitary lamp,
       To brave the night
And walking from his Sun, when past
       That glim'ring Ray
Cuts through the heavy mists in haste
       Back to his day,
So o'r fled minutes I retreat
       Unto that hour
Which shew'd thee last, but did defeat
       Thy light, and pow'r,
I search, and rack my soul to see
       Those beams again,
But nothing but the snuff to me
       Appeareth plain;
That dark, and dead sleeps in its known,
       And common urn,
But those fled to their Makers throne,
       There shine, and burn;
O could I track them! but souls must
       Track one the other,
And now the spirit, not the dust
       Must be thy brother.
Yet I have one *Pearle* by whose light
       All things I see,
And in the heart of Earth, and night
       Find Heaven, and thee.

¶

Sure, there's a tye of Bodyes! and as they
　　　Dissolve (with it,) to Clay,
Love languisheth, and memory doth rust
　　　O'r-cast with that cold dust;
For things thus *Center'd* without *Beames*, or *Action*
　　　Nor give, nor take *Contaction*,
And man is such a Marygold, these fled,
　　　That shuts, and hangs the head.

2

Absents within the Line Conspire, and *Sense*
　　　Things distant doth unite,
Herbs sleep unto the *East*, and some fowles thence
　　　Watch the Returns of light;
But hearts are not so kind: false, short delights
　　　Tell us the world is brave,
And wrap us in Imaginary flights
　　　Wide of a faithfull grave;
Thus *Lazarus* was carried out of town;
　　　For 'tis our foes chief art
By distance all good objects first to drown,
　　　And then besiege the heart.
But I will be my own *Deaths-head*; and though
　　　The flatt'rer say, *I live*,
Because Incertainties we cannot know
　　　Be sure, not to believe.

Peace

My Soul, there is a Countrie
    Far beyond the stars,
Where stands a winged Centrie
    All skilfull in the wars,
There above noise, and danger
    Sweet peace sits crown'd with smiles,
And one born in a Manger
    Commands the Beauteous files,
He is thy gracious friend,
    And (O my Soul awake!)
Did in pure love descend
    To die here for thy sake,
If thou canst get but thither,
    There growes the flowre of peace,
The Rose that cannot wither,
    Thy fortresse, and thy ease;
Leave then thy foolish ranges;
    For none can thee secure,
But one, who never changes,
    Thy God, thy life, thy Cure.

Romans 8.19

Etenim res Creatæ exerto Capite observantes expectant revelationem
Filiorum Dei.

And do they so? have they a Sense
    Of ought but Influence?
Can they their heads lift, and expect,
    And grone too? why th'Elect
Can do no more: my volumes sed
    They were all dull, and dead,
They judg'd them senslesse, and their state
    Wholly Inanimate.
    Go, go; Seal up thy looks,
      And burn thy books.

2

I would I were a stone, or tree,
    Or flowre by pedigree,
Or some poor high-way herb, or Spring
    To flow, or bird to sing!
Then should I (tyed to one sure state,)
    All day expect my date;
But I am sadly loose, and stray
    A giddy blast each way;
    O let me not thus range!
      Thou canst not change.

3

Sometimes I sit with thee, and tarry
    An hour, or so, then vary.
Thy other Creatures in this Scene
    Thee only aym, and mean;
Some rise to seek thee, and with heads
    Erect peep from their beds;
Others, whose birth is in the tomb,
    And cannot quit the womb,

Sigh there, and grone for thee,
　　Their liberty.

4

O let not me do lesse! shall they
　　Watch, while I sleep, or play?
Shall I thy mercies still abuse
　　With fancies, friends, or newes?
O brook it not! thy bloud is mine,
　　And my soul should be thine;
O brook it not! why wilt thou stop
　　After whole showres one drop?
Sure, thou wilt joy to see
　　Thy sheep with thee.

The Relapse

My God, how gracious art thou! I had slipt
   Almost to hell,
And on the verge of that dark, dreadful pit
   Did hear them yell,
But O thy love! thy rich, almighty love
   That sav'd my soul,
And checkt their furie, when I saw them move,
   And heard them howl;
O my sole Comfort, take no more these wayes,
   This hideous path,
And I wil mend my own without delayes,
   Cease thou thy wrath!
I have deserv'd a thick, Egyptian damp,
   Dark as my deeds,
Should *mist* within me, and put out that lamp
   Thy spirit feeds;
A darting Conscience full of stabs, and fears;
   No shade but *Yewgh*,
Sullen, and sad Ecclipses, Cloudie spheres,
   These are my due.
But he that with his bloud, (a price too deere,)
   My scores did pay,
Bid me, by vertue from him, chalenge here
   The brightest day;
Sweet, downie thoughts; soft *Lilly*-shades; Calm streams;
   Joyes full, and true;
Fresh, spicie mornings; and eternal beams
   These are his due.

The Resolve

I have consider'd it; and find
        A longer stay
Is but excus'd neglect. To mind
        One path, and stray
Into another, or to none,
        Cannot be love;
When shal that traveller come home,
        That will not move?
If thou wouldst thither, linger not,
        Catch at the place,
Tell youth and beauty they must rot,
        They'r but a *Case*;
Loose, parcell'd hearts wil freeze: The Sun
        With scatter'd locks
Scarce warms, but by contraction
        Can heat rocks;
Call in thy *Powers*; run, and reach
        Home with the light,
Be there, before the shadows stretch,
        And *Span* up night;
Follow the *Cry* no more: there is
        An ancient way
All strewed with flowres, and happiness
        And fresh as *May*;
There turn, and turn no more; Let wits,
        Smile at fair eies,
Or lips; But who there weeping sits,
        Hath got the *Prize*.

The Match

Dear friend! whose holy, ever-living lines
    Have done much good
   To many, and have checkt my blood,
My fierce, wild blood that still heaves, and inclines,
    But is still tam'd
   By those bright fires which thee inflam'd;
Here I joyn hands, and thrust my stubborn heart
    Into thy *Deed*,
   There from no *Duties* to be freed,
And if hereafter *youth*, or *folly* thwart
    And claim their share,
   Here I renounce the pois'nous ware.

II

Accept, dread Lord, the poor Oblation,
    It is but poore,
   Yet through thy Mercies may be more.
O thou! that canst not wish my souls damnation,
    Afford me life,
   And save me from all inward strife!
Two *Lifes* I hold from thee, my gracious Lord,
    Both cost thee deer,
   For one, I am thy Tenant here;
The other, the true life, in the next world
    And endless is,
   O let me still mind *that* in *this*!
To thee therefore my *Thoughts*, *Words*, *Actions*
    I do resign,
   Thy will in all be done, not mine.
Settle my *house*, and shut out all distractions
    That may unknit
   My heart, and thee planted in it;
Lord *Jesu*! thou didst bow thy blessed head
    Upon a tree,

O do as much, now unto me!
O hear, and heal thy servant! Lord, strike dead
All lusts in me,
Who onely wish life to serve thee?
Suffer no more this dust to overflow
And drown my eies,
But seal, or pin them to thy skies.
And let this *grain* which here in tears I sow
Though *dead* and *sick*,
Through thy *Increase* grow *new*, and *quick*.

Rules *and* Lessons

When first thy Eies unveil, give thy Soul leave
To do the like; our Bodies but forerun
The spirits duty; True hearts spread, and heave
Unto their God, as flow'rs do to the Sun.
     Give him thy first thoughts then; so shalt thou keep
     Him company all day, and in him sleep.

Yet, never sleep the Sun up; Prayer shou'd
Dawn with the day; There are set, awful hours
'Twix heaven, and us; The *Manna* was not good
After Sun-rising, far-day sullies flowres.
     Rise to prevent the Sun; sleep doth sins glut,
     And heav'ns gate opens, when this world's is shut.

Walk with thy fellow-creatures: note the *hush*
And *whispers* amongst them. There's not a *Spring*,
Or *Leafe* but hath his *Morning-hymn*; Each *Bush*
And *Oak* doth know *I AM*; canst thou not sing?
     O leave thy Cares, and follies! go this way
     And thou art sure to prosper all the day.

Serve God before the world; let him not go
Until thou hast a blessing, then resigne
The whole unto him; and remember who
Prevail'd by *wrestling* ere the *Sun* did *shine*.
     Poure *Oyle* upon the *stones*, weep for thy sin,
     Then journey on, and have an eie to heav'n.

Mornings are *Mysteries*; the first worlds *Youth*,
Mans *Resurrection*, and the futures *Bud*
Shrowd in their births: The Crown of life, light, truth
Is stil'd their *starre*, the *stone*, and *hidden food*.
     Three *blessings* wait upon them, two of which
     Should move; They make us *holy, happy*, rich.

When the world's up, and ev'ry swarm abroad,
Keep thou thy temper, mix not with each Clay;
Dispatch necessities, life hath a load
Which must be carri'd on, and safely may.
  Yet keep those cares without thee, let the heart
  Be Gods alone, and choose the better part.

Through all thy *Actions, Counsels,* and *Discourse,*
Let *Mildness,* and *Religion* guide thee out,
If truth be thine, what needs a brutish force?
But what's not *good,* and *just* ne'r go about.
  Wrong not thy Conscience for a rotten stick,
  That gain is dreadful, which makes spirits sick.

To God, thy Countrie, and thy friend be true,
If *Priest,* and *People* change, keep thou thy ground.
Who sels Religion, is a *Judas Jew,*
And, oathes once broke, the soul cannot be sound.
  The perjurer's a devil let loose: what can
  Tie up his hands, that dares mock God, and man?

Seek not the same steps with the *Crowd*; stick thou
To thy sure trot; a Constant, humble mind
Is both his own Joy, and his Makers too;
Let folly dust it on, or lag behind.
  A sweet *self-privacy* in a right soul
  Out-runs the Earth, and lines the utmost pole.

To all that seek thee, bear an open heart;
Make not thy breast a *Labyrinth,* or *Trap*;
If tryals come, this wil make good thy part,
For honesty is safe, come what can hap;
  It is the good mans *feast*; The prince of flowres
  Which thrives in *storms,* and smels best after *showres.*

Seal not thy Eyes up from the poor, but give
Proportion to their *Merits,* and thy *Purse*;
Thou mai'st in Rags a mighty Prince relieve

Who, when thy sins call for't, can fence a Curse.
    Thou shalt not lose one *mite*. Though waters stray,
    The Bread we cast returns in fraughts one day.

Spend not an hour so, as to weep another,
For tears are not thine own; If thou giv'st words
Dash not thy *friend*, nor *Heav'n*; O smother
A vip'rous thought; some *Syllables* are *Swords*.
    Unbitted tongues are in their penance double,
    They shame their *owners*, and the *hearers* trouble.

Injure not modest bloud, whose *spirits* rise
In judgement against *Lewdness*; that's base wit
That voyds but *filth*, and *stench*. Hast thou no prize
But *sickness*, or *Infection*? stifle it.
    Who makes his jests of sins, must be at least
    If not a very *devill*, worse than a *Beast*.

Yet, fly no friend, if he be such indeed,
But meet to quench his *Longings*, and thy *Thirst*;
Allow your Joyes *Religion*; That done, speed
And bring the same man back, thou wert at first.
    Who so returns not, cannot pray aright,
    But shuts his door, and leaves God out all night.

To highten thy *Devotions*, and keep low
All mutinous thoughts, what busines e'r thou hast
Observe God in his works; here *fountains* flow,
Birds sing, *Beasts* feed, *Fish* leap, and th'*Earth* stands fast;
    Above are restles *motions*, running *Lights*,
    Vast Circling *Azure*, giddy *Clouds*, days, nights.

When *Seasons* change, then lay before thine Eys
His wondrous *Method*; mark the various *Scenes*
In heav'n; *Hail*, *Thunder*, *Rain-bows*, *Snow*, and *Ice*,
Calmes, *Tempests*, *Light*, and *darknes* by his means;
    Thou canst not misse his Praise; Each *tree, herb, flowre*
    Are shadows of his *wisedome*, and his Pow'r.

To *meales* when thou doest come, give him the praise
Whose *Arm* supply'd thee; Take what may suffice,
And then be thankful; O admire his ways
Who fils the worlds unempty'd granaries!
    A thankles feeder is a *Theif*, his feast
    A very *Robbery*, and himself no *guest*.

High-noon thus past, thy time decays; provide
Thee other thoughts; Away with friends, and mirth;
The Sun now stoops, and hasts his beams to hide
Under the dark, and melancholy Earth.
    All but preludes thy End. Thou art the man
    Whose *Rise*, *hight*, and *Descent* is but a span.

Yet, set as he doth, and 'tis well. Have all
Thy Beams home with thee: trim thy *Lamp*, buy *Oyl*,
And then set forth; who is thus drest, The *Fall*
Furthers his glory, and gives death the foyl.
    Man is a *Summers day*; whose *youth*, and *fire*
    Cool to a glorious *Evening*, and Expire.

When night comes, list thy deeds; make plain the way
'Twix Heaven, and thee; block it not with delays,
But perfect all before thou sleep'st; Then say
Ther's one Sun more strung on my Bead of days.
    What's good score up for Joy; The bad wel scann'd
    Wash off with tears, and get thy *Masters* hand.

Thy Accounts thus made, spend in the grave one houre
Before thy time; Be not a stranger there
Where thou may'st sleep whole ages; Lifes poor flowr
Lasts not a night sometimes. Bad spirits fear
    This Conversation; But the good man lyes
    Intombed many days before he dyes.

Being laid, and drest for sleep, Close not thy Eys
Up with thy Curtains; Give thy soul the wing
In some good thoughts; So when the day shall rise

And thou *unrak'st* thy *fire*, those *sparks* will bring
    New *flames*; Besides where these lodge vain *heats* mourn
    And die; That *Bush* where God is, shall not burn.

When thy *Nap's* over, stir thy fire, unrake
In that *dead age*; one beam i'th' dark outvies
Two in the day; Then from the *Damps*, and *Ake*
Of night shut up thy *leaves*, be Chast; God prys
    Through thickest nights; Though then the Sun be far
    Do thou the works of *Day*, and rise a *Star*.

Briefly, *Doe as thou would'st be done unto,*
Love God, and Love thy Neighbour; Watch, and Pray.
These are the *Words*, and *Works* of life; This do,
And live; who doth not thus, hath lost *Heav'ns way.*
    O lose it not! look up, wilt Change those *Lights*
    For *Chains* of *Darknes*, and *Eternal Nights*?

Corruption

Sure, It was so. Man in those early days
    Was not all stone, and Earth,
He shin'd a little, and by those weak Rays
    Had some glimpse of his birth.
He saw Heaven o'r his head, and knew from whence
    He came (condemned,) hither,
And, as first Love draws strongest, so from hence
    His mind sure progress'd thither.
Things here were strange unto him: Swet, and till
    All was a thorn, or weed,
Nor did those last, but (like himself,) dyed still
    As soon as they did *Seed*,
They seem'd to quarrel with him; for that Act
    That fel him, foyl'd them all,
He drew the Curse upon the world, and Crackt
    The whole frame with his fall.
This made him long for *home*, as loath to stay
    With murmurers, and foes;
He sigh'd for *Eden*, and would often say
    Ah! what bright days were those?
Nor was Heav'n cold unto him; for each day
    The vally, or the Mountain
Afforded visits, and still *Paradise* lay
    In some green shade, or fountain.
Angels lay *Leiger* here; Each Bush, and Cel,
    Each Oke, and high-way knew them,
Walk but the fields, or sit down at some *wel*,
    And he was sure to view them.
Almighty *Love*! where art thou now? mad man
    Sits down, and freezeth on,
He raves, and swears to stir nor fire, nor fan,
    But bids the thread be spun.
I see, thy Curtains are Close-drawn; Thy bow
    Looks dim too in the Cloud,

Sin triumphs still, and man is sunk below
    The Center, and his shrowd;
All's in deep sleep, and night; Thick darknes lyes
    And hatcheth o'r thy people;
But hark! what trumpets that? what Angel cries
    Arise! Thrust in thy sickle.

Unprofitablenes

How rich, O Lord! how fresh thy visits are!
'Twas but Just now my bleak leaves hopeles hung
     Sullyed with dust and mud;
Each snarling blast shot through me, and did share
Their Youth, and beauty, Cold showres nipt, and wrung
     Their spiciness, and bloud;
But since thou didst in one sweet glance survey
Their sad decays, I flourish, and once more
     Breath all perfumes, and spice;
I smell a dew like *Myrrh*, and all the day
Wear in my bosome a full Sun; such store
     Hath one beame from thy Eys.
But, ah, my God! what fruit hast thou of this?
What one poor leaf did ever I yet fall
     To wait upon thy wreath?
Thus thou all day a thankless weed doest dress,
And when th' hast done, a stench, or fog is all
     The odour I bequeath.

Christs Nativity

I

Awake, glad heart! get up, and Sing,
It is the Birth-day of thy King,
    Awake! awake!
    The Sun doth shake
Light from his locks, and all the way
Breathing Perfumes, doth spice the day.

2

Awak, awak! heark, how th' *wood* rings,
Winds whisper, and the busie *springs*
    A Consort make;
    Awake, awake!
Man is their high-priest, and should rise
To offer up the sacrifice.

3

I would I were some *Bird*, or Star,
Flutt'ring in woods, or lifted far
    Above this *Inne*
    And Rode of sin!
Then either Star, or *Bird*, should be
Shining, or singing still to thee.

4

I would I had in my best part
Fit Roomes for thee! or that my heart
    Were so clean as
    Thy manger was!
But I am all filth, and obscene,
Yet, if thou wilt, thou canst make clean.

5

Sweet *Jesu*! will then; Let no more
This Leper haunt, and soyl thy door,
　　Cure him, Ease him
　　O release him!
And let once more by mystick birth
The Lord of life be borne in Earth.

II

How kind is heav'n to man! If here
　　One sinner doth amend
Strait there is Joy, and ev'ry sphere
　　In musick doth Contend;
And shall we then no voices lift?
　　Are mercy, and salvation
Not worth our thanks? Is life a gift
　　Of no more acceptation?
Shal he that did come down from thence,
　　And here for us was slain,
Shal he be now cast off? no sense
　　Of all his woes remain?
Can neither Love, nor suff'rings bind?
　　Are we all stone, and Earth?
Neither his bloudy passions mind,
　　Nor one day blesse his birth?
Alas, my God! Thy birth now here
Must not be numbred in the year.

The Check

Peace, peace! I blush to hear thee; when thou art
    A dusty story
A speechlesse heap, and in the midst my heart
    In the same livery drest
    Lyes tame as all the rest;
When six years thence digg'd up, some youthfull Eie
    Seeks there for Symmetry
But finding none, shal leave thee to the wind,
    Or the next foot to Crush,
    Scatt'ring thy kind
    And humble dust, tell then dear flesh
    Where is thy glory?

2

As he that in the midst of day Expects
    The hideous night,
Sleeps not, but shaking off sloth, and neglects,
    Works with the Sun, and sets
    Paying the day its debts;
That (for Repose, and darknes bound,) he might
    Rest from the fears i'th' night;
So should we too. All things teach us to die
    And point us out the way
    While we passe by
    And mind it not; play not away
    Thy glimpse of light.

3

View thy fore runners: Creatures giv'n to be
    Thy youths Companions,
Take their leave, and die; Birds, beasts, each tree
    All that have growth, or breath
    Have one large language, *Death*.
O then play not! but strive to him, who Can

Make these sad shades pure Sun,
Turning their mists to beams, their damps to day,
    Whose pow'r doth so excell
        As to make Clay
    A spirit, and true glory dwell
        In dust, and stones.

4

Heark, how he doth Invite thee! with what voice
        Of Love, and sorrow
He begs, and Calls; *O that in these thy days*
        Thou knew'st but thy own good!
    Shall not the Crys of bloud,
Of Gods own bloud awake thee? He bids beware
        Of drunknes, surfeits, Care,
But thou sleep'st on; wher's now thy protestation,
        Thy Lines, thy Love? Away,
            Redeem the day,
    The day that gives no observation,
        Perhaps to morrow.

Disorder *and* frailty

When first thou didst even from the grave
And womb of darknes becken out
My brutish soul, and to thy slave
Becam'st thy self, both guide, and Scout;
     Even from that hour
Thou gotst my heart; And though here tost
    By winds, and bit with frost
      I pine, and shrink
      Breaking the link
'Twixt thee, and me; And oftimes creep
Into th' old silence, and dead sleep,
      Quitting thy way
      All the long day,
Yet, sure, my God! I love thee most.
     Alas, thy love!

      2
I threaten heaven, and from my Cell
Of Clay, and frailty break, and bud
Touch'd by thy fire, and breath; Thy bloud
Too, is my Dew, and springing wel.
     But while I grow
And stretch to thee, ayming at all
    Thy stars, and spangled hall,
      Each fly doth tast,
      Poyson, and blast
My yielding leaves; sometimes a showr
Beats them quite off, and in an hour
      Not one poor shoot
      But the bare root
Hid under ground survives the fall.
     Alas, frail weed!

3

Thus like some sleeping Exhalation
(Which wak'd by heat, and beams, makes up
Unto that Comforter, the Sun,
And soars, and shines; But e'r we sup
          And walk two steps
Cool'd by the damps of night, descends,
          And, whence it sprung, there ends,)
               Doth my weak fire
               Pine, and retire,
And (after all my hight of flames,)
In sickly Expirations tames
               Leaving me dead
               On my first bed
Untill thy Sun again ascends.
               Poor, falling Star!

4

O, is! but give wings to my fire,
And hatch my soul, untill it fly
Up where thou art, amongst thy tire
Of Stars, above Infirmity;
               Let not perverse,
And foolish thoughts adde to my Bil
               Of forward sins, and Kil
               That seed, which thou
               In me didst sow,
But dresse, and water with thy grace
Together with the seed, the place;
               And for his sake
               Who died to stake
His life for mine, tune to thy will
               My heart, my verse.

Hosea 6.4
O Ephraim what shall I do unto thee? O Judah how shall I intreat thee?
for thy goodness is as a morning Cloud, and as the early Dew it goeth away.

Son-dayes

Bright shadows of true Rest! some shoots of blisse,
                                    Heaven once a week;
The next worlds gladnes prepossest in this;
                                    A day to seek
Eternity in time; the steps by which
We Climb above all ages; Lamps that light
Man through his heap of dark days; and the rich,
And full redemption of the whole weeks flight.

2

The Pulleys unto headlong man; times bower;
                                    The narrow way;
Transplanted Paradise; Gods walking houre;
                                    The Cool o'th' day;
The Creatures *Jubile*; Gods parle with dust;
Heaven here; Man on those hills of Myrrh, and flowres;
Angels descending; the Returns of Trust;
A Gleam of glory, after six-days-showres.

3

The Churches love-feasts; Times Prerogative,
                                    And Interest
Deducted from the whole; The Combs, and hive,
                                    And home of rest.
The milky way Chalkt out with Suns; a Clue
That guides through erring hours; and in full story
A taste of Heav'n on earth; the pledge, and Cue
Of a full feast; And the Out Courts of glory.

Repentance

Lord, since thou didst in this vile Clay
    That sacred Ray
Thy spirit plant, quickning the whole
With that one grains Infused wealth,
My forward flesh creept on, and subtly stole
Both growth, and power; Checking the health
And heat of thine: That little gate
And narrow way, by which to thee
The Passage is, He term'd a grate
And Entrance to Captivitie;
Thy laws but nets, where some small birds
(And those but seldome too) were caught,
Thy Promises but empty words
Which none but Children heard, or taught.
This I believed: And though a friend
Came oft from far, and whisper'd, *No*;
Yet that not sorting to my end
I wholy listen'd to my foe.
Wherefore, pierc'd through with grief, my sad
Seduced soul sighs up to thee,
To thee who with true light art Clad
And seest all things just as they be.
Look from thy throne upon this Rowl
Of heavy sins, my high transgressions,
Which I Confesse withall my soul,
My God, Accept of my Confession.
    It was last day
(Touch'd with the guilt of my own way)
I sate alone, and taking up
    The bitter Cup,
Through all thy fair, and various store
Sought out what might outvie my score.
    The blades of grasse, thy Creatures feeding,
    The trees, their leafs; the flowres, their seeding;

The Dust, of which I am a part,
The Stones much softer than my heart,
The drops of rain, the sighs of wind,
The Stars to which I am stark blind,
The Dew thy herbs drink up by night,
The beams they warm them at i'th' light,
All that have signature or life,
I summon'd to decide this strife,
And lest I should lack for Arrears,
A spring ran by, I told her tears,
But when these came unto the scale,
My sins alone outweigh'd them all.
O my dear God! my life, my love!
Most blessed lamb! and mildest dove!
Forgive your penitent Offender,
And no more his sins remember,
Scatter these shades of death, and give
Light to my soul, that it may live;
Cut me not off for my transgressions,
Wilful rebellions, and suppressions,
But give them in those streams a part
Whose spring is in my Saviours heart.
Lord, I confesse the heynous score,
And pray, I may do so no more,
Though then all sinners I exceed
O think on this; *Thy Son did bleed;*
O call to mind his wounds, his woes,
His Agony, and bloudy throws;
Then look on all that thou hast made,
And mark how they do fail, and fade,
The heavens themselves, though fair and bright
Are dark, and unclean in thy sight,
How then, with thee, Can man be holy
Who doest thine Angels charge with folly?
O what am I, that I should breed
Figs on a thorne, flowres on a weed!

I am the gourd of sin, and sorrow
Growing o'r night, and gone to morrow,
In all this *Round* of life and death
Nothing's more vile than is my breath,
Profanenes on my tongue doth rest,
Defects, and darknes in my brest,
Pollutions all my body wed,
And even my soul to thee is dead,
Only in him, on whom I feast,
Both soul, and body are well drest,
    His pure perfection quits all score,
    And fills the Boxes of his poor;
He is the Center of long life, and light,
I am but finite, He is Infinite.
O let thy *Justice* then in him Confine,
And through his merits, make thy mercy mine!

The Dawning

Ah! what time wilt thou come? when shall that crie
　　The *Bridegroome's Comming*! fil the sky?
　　Shall it in the Evening run
　　When our words and works are done?
　　Or wil thy all-surprizing light
　　　　Break at midnight?
When either sleep, or some dark pleasure
Possesseth mad man without measure;
Or shal these early, fragrant hours
　　Unlock thy bowres?
And with their blush of light descry
Thy locks crown'd with eternitie;
Indeed, it is the only time
That with thy glory doth best chime,
All now are stirring, ev'ry field
　　Ful hymns doth yield,
The whole Creation shakes off night,
And for thy shadow looks the light,
Stars now vanish without number,
Sleepie Planets set, and slumber,
The pursie Clouds disband, and scatter,
All expect some sudden matter,
Not one beam triumphs, but from far
　　That morning-star;
O at what time soever thou
(Unknown to us,) the heavens wilt bow,
And, with thy Angels in the *Van*,
Descend to Judge poor careless man,
Grant, I may not like puddle lie
In a Corrupt securitie,
Where, if a traveller water crave,
He finds it dead, and in a grave;
But as this restless, vocall *Spring*
All day, and night doth run, and sing,

And though here born, yet is acquainted
Elsewhere, and flowing keeps untainted;
So let me all my busie age
In thy free services ingage,
And though (while here) of force I must
Have Commerce somtimes with poor dust,
And in my flesh, though vile, and low,
As this doth in her Channel, flow,
Yet let my Course, my aym, my Love,
And chief acquaintance be above;
So when that day, and hour shal come
In which thy self wil be the Sun,
Thou'lt find me drest and on my way,
Watching the Break of thy great day.

Dressing

O thou that lovest a pure, and whitend soul!
That feedst among the Lillies, 'till the day
Break, and the shadows flee; touch with one Coal
My frozen heart; and with thy secret key

Open my desolate rooms; my gloomie Brest
With thy cleer fire refine, burning to dust
These dark Confusions, that within me nest,
And soyl thy Temple with a sinful rust.

Thou holy, harmless, undefil'd high-priest!
The perfect, ful oblation for all sin,
Whose glorious conquest nothing can resist,
But even in babes doest triumph still and win;

    Give to thy wretched one
  Thy mysticall *Communion*,
      That, absent, he may see,
      Live, die, and rise with thee;
Let him so follow here, that in the end
He may take thee, as thou doest him intend.
    Give him thy private seal,
  Earnest, and sign; Thy gifts so deal
      That these forerunners here
      May make the future cleer;
Whatever thou dost bid, let faith make good,
Bread for thy body, and Wine for thy blood.
    Give him (with pitty) love,
  Two flowres that grew with thee above;
      Love that shal not admit
      Anger for one short fit,
And pitty of such a divine extent
That may thy members, more than mine, resent.

    Give me, my God! thy grace,
  The beams, and brightnes of thy face,

That never like a beast
I take thy sacred feast,
Or the dread mysteries of thy blest bloud
Use, with like Custome, as my Kitchin food.
Some sit to thee, and eat
Thy body as their Common meat,
O let not me do so!
Poor dust should ly still low,
Then kneel my soul, and body; kneel, and bow;
If *Saints*, and *Angels* fal down, much more thou.

The Holy Communion

Welcome sweet, and sacred feast; welcome life!
    Dead I was, and deep in trouble;
But grace, and blessings came with thee so rife,
That they have quicken'd even drie stubble;
      Thus soules their bodies animate,
        And thus, at first, when things were rude,
          Dark, void, and Crude
They, by thy Word, their beauty had, and date;
        All were by thee,
        And stil must be,
     Nothing that is, or lives,
But hath his Quicknings, and reprieves
    As thy hand opes, or shuts;
      Healings, and Cuts,
Darkness, and day-light, life, and death
Are but meer leaves turn'd by thy breath.
    Spirits without thee die,
      And blackness sits
    On the divinest wits,
As on the Sun Ecclipses lie.
But that great darkness at thy death
When the veyl broke with thy last breath,
      Did make us see
      The way to thee;
And now by these sure, sacred ties.
      After thy blood
      (Our sov'rain good,)
      Had clear'd our eies,
      And given us sight;
Thou dost unto thy self betroth
   Our souls, and bodies both
   In everlasting light.

Was't not enough that thou hadst payd the price
And given us eies
When we had none, but thou must also take
Us by the hand
And keep us still awake,
When we would sleep,
Or from thee creep,
Who without thee cannot stand?

Was't not enough to lose thy breath
And blood by an accursed death,
But thou must also leave
To us that did bereave
Thee of them both, these seals the means
That should both cleanse
And keep us so,
Who wrought thy wo?
O rose of *Sharon*! O the Lilly
Of the valley!
How art thou now, thy flock to keep,
Become both *food*, and *Shepheard* to thy sheep.

Affliction

Peace, peace; It is not so. Thou doest miscall
    Thy Physick; Pils that change
Thy sick Accessions into setled health,
This is the great *Elixir* that turns gall
To wine, and sweetness; Poverty to wealth,
   And brings man home, when he doth range.
   Did not he, who ordain'd the day,
       Ordain night too?
   And in the greater world display
   What in the lesser he would do?
All flesh is Clay, thou know'st; and but that God
    Doth use his rod,
And by a fruitfull Change of frosts, and showres
    Cherish, and bind thy *pow'rs*,
Thou wouldst to weeds, and thistles quite disperse,
    And be more wild than is thy verse;
Sickness is wholsome, and Crosses are but curbs
    To check the mule, unruly man,
They are heavens husbandry, the famous fan
    Purging the floor which Chaff disturbs.
Were all the year one constant Sun-shine, wee
    Should have no flowres,
All would be drought, and leanness; not a tree
    Would make us bowres;
Beauty consists in colours; and that's best
    Which is not fixt, but flies, and flowes;
The settled *Red* is dull, and *whites* that rest
    Something of sickness would disclose.
    Vicissitude plaies all the game,
      Nothing that stirrs,
      Or hath a name,
   But waits upon this wheel,
Kingdomes too have their Physick, and for steel,
    Exchange their peace, and furrs.

Thus doth God *Key* disorder'd man
(Which none else can,)
Tuning his brest to rise, or fall:
And by a sacred, needfull art
Like strings, stretch ev'ry part
Making the whole most Musicall.

The World

I saw Eternity the other night
Like a great *Ring* of pure and endless light,
    All calm, as it was bright,
And round beneath it, Time in hours, days, years
      Driv'n by the spheres
Like a vast shadow mov'd, In which the world
      And all her train were hurl'd;
The doting Lover in his queintest strain
      Did their Complain,
Neer him, his Lute, his fancy, and his flights,
      Wits sour delights,
With gloves, and knots the silly snares of pleasure
      Yet his dear Treasure
All scatter'd lay, while he his eys did pour
      Upon a flowr.

2

The darksome States-man hung with weights and woe
Like a thick midnight-fog mov'd there so slow
    He did nor stay, nor go;
Condemning thoughts (like sad Ecclipses) scowl
      Upon his soul,
And Clouds of crying witnesses without
      Pursued him with one shout.
Yet dig'd the Mole, and lest his ways be found
      Workt under ground,
Where he did Clutch his prey, but one did see
      That policie,
Churches and altars fed him, Perjuries
      Were gnats and flies,
It rain'd about him bloud and tears, but he
      Drank them as free.

3

The fearfull miser on a heap of rust
Sate pining all his life there, did scarce trust
      His own hands with the dust,
Yet would not place one peece above, but lives
            In feare of theeves.
Thousands there were as frantick as himself
            And hug'd each one his pelf,
The down-right Epicure plac'd heav'n in sense
            And scornd pretence
While others slipt into a wide Excesse
            Said little lesse;
The weaker sort slight, triviall wares Inslave
            Who think them brave,
And poor, despised truth sate Counting by
            Their victory.

4

Yet some, who all this while did weep and sing,
And sing, and weep, soar'd up into the *Ring*,
      But most would use no wing.
O fools (said I,) thus to prefer dark night
            Before true light,
To live in grots, and caves, and hate the day
            Because it shews the way,
The way which from this dead and dark abode
            Leads up to God,
A way where you might tread the Sun, and be
            More bright than he.
But as I did their madnes so discusse
            One whisper'd thus,
This Ring the Bride-groome did for none provide
            But for his bride.

John 2.16–17

All that is in the world, the lust of the flesh, the lust of the Eys,
and the pride of life, is not of the father, but is of the world.
And the world passeth away, and the lusts thereof, but he that
doth the will of God abideth for ever.

The Constellation

Fair, order'd lights (whose motion without noise
    Resembles those true Joys
Whose spring is on that hil where you do grow
    And we here tast sometimes below,)

With what exact obedience do you move
    Now beneath, and now above,
And in your vast progressions overlook
    The darkest night, and closest nook!

Some nights I see you in the gladsome East,
    Some others neer the West,
And when I cannot see, yet do you shine
    And beat about your endles line.

Silence, and light, and watchfulnes with you
    Attend and wind the Clue,
No sleep, nor sloth assailes you, but poor man
    Still either sleeps, or slips his span.

He grops beneath here, and with restless Care
    First makes, then hugs a snare,
Adores dead dust, sets heart on Corne and grass
    But seldom doth make heav'n his glass.

Musick and mirth (if there be musick here)
    Take up, and tune his year,
These things are Kin to him, and must be had,
    Who kneels, or sighs a life is mad.

Perhaps some nights hee'l watch with you, and peep
    When it were best to sleep,
Dares know Effects, and Judge them long before,
    When th' herb he treads knows much, much more.

But seeks he your *Obedience, Order, Light,*
    Your calm and wel-train'd flight,
Where, though the glory differ in each star,
    Yet is there peace still, and no war?

Since plac'd by him who calls you by your names
    And fixt there all your flames,
Without Command you never acted ought
    And then you in your Courses fought.

But here Commission'd by a black self-wil
    The sons the father kil,
The Children Chase the mother, and would heal
    The wounds they give, by crying, zeale.

Then Cast her bloud, and tears upon thy book
    Where they for fashion look,
And like that Lamb which had the Dragons voice
    Seem mild, but are known by their noise.

Thus by our lusts disorder'd into wars
    Our guides prove wandring stars,
Which for these mists, and black days were reserv'd,
    What time we from our first love swerv'd.

Yet O for his sake who sits now by thee
    All crown'd with victory,
So guide us through this Darknes, that we may
    Be more and more in love with day;

Settle, and fix our hearts, that we may move
    In order, peace, and love,
And taught obedience by thy whole Creation,
    Become an humble, holy nation.

Give to thy spouse her perfect, and pure dress,
    Beauty and *holiness,*
And so repair these Rents, that men may see
    And say, *Where God is, all agree.*

Misery

Lord, bind me up, and let me lye
A Pris'ner to my libertie,
If such a state at all can be
As an Impris'ment serving thee;
The wind, though gather'd in thy fist,
Yet doth it blow stil where it list,
And yet shouldst thou let go thy hold
Those gusts might quarrel and grow bold.
    As waters here, headlong and loose
The lower grounds stil chase, and choose,
Where spreading all the way they seek
And search out ev'ry hole, and Creek;
So my spilt thoughts winding from thee
Take the down-rode to vanitie,
Where they all stray and strive, which shal
Find out the first and steepest fal;
I cheer their flow, giving supply
To what's already grown too high,
And having thus perform'd that part
Feed on those vomits of my heart.
I break the fence my own hands made
Then lay that trespasse in the shade,
Some fig-leafs stil I do devise
As if thou hadst nor ears, nor Eyes.
Excesse of friends, of words, and wine
Take up my day, while thou dost shine
All unregarded, and thy book
Hath not so much as one poor look.
If thou steal in amidst the mirth
And kindly tel me, *I am Earth*,
I shut thee out, and let that slip,
Such Musick spoils good fellowship.
Thus wretched I, and most unkind,
Exclude my dear God from my mind,

Exclude him thence, who of that Cel
Would make a Court, should he there dwel.
He goes, he yields; And troubled sore
His holy spirit grieves therefore,
The mighty God, th' eternal King
Doth grieve for Dust, and Dust doth sing.
But I go on, haste to Devest
My self of reason, till opprest
And buried in my surfeits I
Prove my own shame and miserie.
Next day I call and cry for thee
Who shouldst not then come neer to me,
But now it is thy servants pleasure
Thou must (and dost) give him his measure.
Thou dost, thou com'st, and in a showr
Of healing sweets thy self dost powr
Into my wounds, and now thy grace
(I know it wel,) fils all the place;
I sit with thee by this new light,
And for that hour th'art my delight,
No man can more the world despise
Or thy great mercies better prize.
I School my Eys, and strictly dwel
Within the Circle of my Cel,
That Calm and silence are my Joys
Which to thy peace are but meer noise.
At length I feel my head to ake,
My fingers Itch, and burn to take
Some new Imployment, I begin
To swel and fome and fret within.
 '*The Age, the present times are not*
 To snudge in, and embrace a Cot,
 Action and bloud now get the game,
 Disdein treads on the peaceful name,
 Who sits at home too bears a loade
 Greater than those that gad abroad.'

Thus do I make thy gifts giv'n me
The only quarrellers with thee,
I'd loose those knots thy hands did tie,
Then would go travel, fight or die.
Thousands of wild and waste Infusions
Like waves beat on my resolutions,
As flames about their fuel run
And work, and wind til all be done,
So my fierce soul bustles about
And never rests til all be out.
Thus wilded by a peevish heart
Which in thy musick bears no part
I storm at thee, calling my peace
A Lethargy, and meer disease,
Nay, those bright beams shot from thy eys
To calm me in these mutinies
I stile meer tempers, which take place
At some set times, but are thy grace.
    Such is mans life; and such is mine
The worst of men, and yet stil thine,
Stil thine thou know'st, and if not so
Then give me over to my foe.
Yet since as easie 'tis for thee
To make man good, as bid him be,
And with one glaunce (could he that gain,)
To look him out of all his pain,
O send me from thy holy hil
So much of strength, as may fulfil
All thy delight (what e'r they be)
And sacred Institutes in me;
Open my rockie heart, and fil
It with obedience to thy wil,
Then seal it up, that as none see,
So none may enter there but thee.
    O hear my God! hear him, whose bloud
Speaks more and better for my good!

O let my Crie come to thy throne!
My crie not pour'd with tears alone,
(For tears alone are often foul)
But with the bloud of all my soul,
With spirit-sighs, and earnest grones,
Faithful and most repenting mones,
With these I crie, and crying pine
Till thou both mend and make me thine.

The Sap

Come sapless Blossom, creep not stil on Earth
    Forgetting thy first birth;
'Tis not from dust, or if so, why dost thou
    Thus cal and thirst for dew?
It tends not thither, if it doth, why then
    This growth and stretch for heav'n?
Thy root sucks but diseases, worms there seat
    And claim it for their meat.
Who plac'd thee here, did something then Infuse
    Which now can tel thee news.
There is beyond the Stars an hil of myrrh
    From which some drops fal here,
On it the Prince of *Salem* sits, who deals
    To thee thy secret meals,
There is thy Country, and he is the way
    And hath withal the key.
Yet liv'd he here sometimes, and bore for thee
    A world of miserie,
For thee, who in the first mans loyns didst fal
    From that hil to this vale,
And had not he so done, it is most true
    Two deaths had bin thy due;
But going hence, and knowing wel what woes
    Might his friends discompose,
To shew what strange love he had to our good
    He gave his sacred bloud
By wil our sap, and Cordial; now in this
    Lies such a heav'n of bliss,
That, who but truly tasts it, no decay
    Can touch him any way,
Such secret life, and vertue in it lies
    It wil exalt and rise
And actuate such spirits as are shed
    Or ready to be dead,

And bring new too. Get then this sap, and get
    Good store of it, but let
The vessel where you put it be for sure
    To all your pow'r most pure;
There is at all times (though shut up) in you
    A powerful, rare dew,
Which only grief and love extract; with this
    Be sure, and never miss,
To wash your vessel wel: Then humbly take
    This balm for souls that ake,
And one who drank it thus, assures that you
    Shal find a Joy so true,
Such perfect Ease, and such a lively sense
    Of grace against all sins,
That you'l Confess the Comfort such, as even
    Brings to, and comes from Heaven.

Mount of Olives

When first I saw true beauty, and thy Joys
Active as light, and calm without all noise
Shin'd on my soul, I felt through all my powr's
Such a rich air of sweets, as Evening showrs
Fand by a gentle gale Convey and breath
On some parch'd bank, crown'd with a flowrie wreath;
Odors, and Myrrh, and balm in one rich floud
O'r-ran my heart, and spirited my bloud,
My thoughts did swim in Comforts, and mine eie
Confest, *The world did only paint and lie.*
And where before I did no safe Course steer
But wander'd under tempests all the year,
Went bleak and bare in body as in mind,
And was blow'n through by ev'ry storm and wind,
I am so warm'd now by this glance on me,
That, midst all storms I feel a Ray of thee;
So have I known some beauteous *Paisage* rise
In suddain flowres and arbours to my Eies,
And in the depth and dead of winter bring
To my Cold thoughts a lively sense of spring.
    Thus fed by thee, who dost all beings nourish,
My wither'd leafs again look green and flourish,
I shine and shelter underneath thy wing
Where sick with love I strive thy name to sing,
Thy glorious name! which grant I may so do
That these may be thy *Praise*, and my *Joy* too.

Man

Weighing the stedfastness and state
Of some mean things which here below reside,
Where birds like watchful Clocks the noiseless date
    And Intercourse of times divide,
Where Bees at night get home and hive, and flowrs
        Early, aswel as late,
Rise with the Sun, and set in the same bowrs;

2

I would (said I) my God would give
The staidness of these things to man! for these
To his divine appointments ever cleave,
    And no new business breaks their peace;
The birds nor sow, nor reap, yet sup and dine,
        The flowres without clothes live,
Yet *Solomon* was never drest so fine.

3

Man hath stil either toyes, or Care,
He hath no root, nor to one place is ty'd,
But ever restless and Irregular
    About this Earth doth run and ride,
He knows he hath a home, but scarce knows where,
        He sayes it is so far
That he hath quite forgot how to go there.

4

He knocks at all doors, strays and roams,
Nay hath not so much wit as some stones have
Which in the darkest nights point to their homes,
    By some hid sense their Maker gave;
Man is the shuttle, to whose winding quest
        And passage through these looms
God order'd motion, but ordain'd no rest.

¶

I walkt the other day (to spend my hour)
Into a field
Where I sometimes had seen the soil to yield
A gallant flowre,
But Winter now had ruffled all the bowre
And curious store
I knew there heretofore.

2

Yet I whose search lov'd not to peep and peer
I'th' face of things
Thought with my self, there might be other springs
Besides this here
Which, like cold friends, sees us but once a year,
And so the flowre
Might have some other bowre.

3

Then taking up what I could neerest spie
I digg'd about
That place where I had seen him to grow out,
And by and by
I saw the warm Recluse alone to lie
Where fresh and green
He lived of us unseen.

4

Many a question Intricate and rare
Did I there strow,
But all I could extort was, that he now
Did there repair
Such losses as befel him in this air
And would e'r long
Come forth most fair and young.

5

This past, I threw the Clothes quite o'r his head,
    And stung with fear
Of my own frailty dropt down many a tear
    Upon his bed,
Then sighing whisper'd, *Happy are the dead!*
    What peace doth now
    Rock him asleep below?

6

And yet, how few believe such doctrine springs
    From a poor root
Which all the Winter sleeps here under foot
    And hath no wings
To raise it to the truth, and light of things,
    But is stil trod
    By ev'ry wandring clod.

7

O thou! whose spirit did at first inflame
    And warm the dead,
And by a sacred Incubation fed
    With life this frame
Which once had neither being, forme, nor name,
    Grant I may so
    Thy steps track here below,

8

That in these Masques and shadows I may see
    Thy sacred way,
And by those hid ascents climb to that day
    Which breaks from thee
Who art in all things, though invisibly;
    Shew me thy peace,
    Thy mercy, love, and ease,

9

And from this Care, where dreams and sorrows raign
Lead me above
Where Light, Joy, Leisure, and true Comforts move
Without all pain,
There, hid in thee, shew me his life again
At whose dumbe urn
Thus all the year I mourn.

From *Silex Scintillans II*

Ascension-Hymn

Dust and clay
Mans antient wear!
Here you must stay,
But I elsewhere;
Souls sojourn here, but may not rest;
Who will ascend, must be undrest.

And yet some
That know to die
Before death come,
Walk to the skie
Even in this life; but all such can
Leave behinde them the old Man.

If a star
Should leave the Sphære,
She must first mar
Her flaming wear,
And after fall, for in her dress
Of glory, she cannot transgress.

Man of old
Within the line
Of *Eden* could
Like the Sun shine
All naked, innocent and bright,
And intimate with Heav'n, as light;

But since he
That brightness soil'd,

His garments be
All dark and spoil'd,
And here are left as nothing worth,
Till the Refiners fire breaks forth.

Then comes he!
Whose mighty light
Made his cloathes be
Like Heav'n, all bright;
The Fuller, whose pure blood did flow
To make stain'd man more white then snow.

Hee alone
And none else can
Bring bone to bone
And rebuild man,
And by his all subduing might
Make clay ascend more quick then light.

¶

They are all gone into the world of light!
　　And I alone sit lingring here;
Their very memory is fair and bright,
　　And my sad thoughts doth clear.

It glows and glitters in my cloudy brest
　　Like stars upon some gloomy grove,
Or those faint beams in which this hill is drest,
　　After the Sun's remove.

I see them walking in an Air of glory,
　　Whose light doth trample on my days:
My days, which are at best but dull and hoary,
　　Meer glimering and decays.

O holy hope! and high humility,
　　High as the Heavens above!
These are your walks, and you have shew'd them me
　　To kindle my cold love,

Dear, beauteous death! the Jewel of the Just,
　　Shining nowhere, but in the dark;
What mysteries do lie beyond thy dust;
　　Could man outlook that mark!

He that hath found some fledg'd birds nest, may know
　　At first sight, if the bird be flown;
But what fair Well, or Grove he sings in now,
　　That is to him unknown.

And yet, as Angels in some brighter dreams
　　Call to the soul, when man doth sleep:
So some strange thoughts transcend our wonted theams,
　　And into glory peep.

If a star were confin'd into a Tomb
　　Her captive flames must needs burn there;

But when the hand that lockt her up, gives room,
    She'l shine through all the sphære.

O Father of eternal life, and all
    Created glories under thee!
Resume thy spirit from this world of thrall
    Into true liberty.

Either disperse these mists, which blot and fill
    My perspective (still) as they pass,
Or else remove me hence unto that hill,
    Where I shall need no glass.

The Proffer

Be still black Parasites,
        Flutter no more;
Were it still winter, as it was before,
        You'd make no flights;
But now the dew and Sun have warm'd my bowres,
    You flie and flock to suck the flowers.

But you would honey make:
        These buds will wither,
And what you now extract, in harder weather
        Will serve to take;
Wise husbands will (you say) there wants prevent,
    Who do not so, too late repent.

O poys'nous, subtile fowls!
        The flyes of hell
That buz in every ear, and blow on souls
        Until they smell
And rot, descend not here, nor think to stay,
    I've read, who 'twas, drove you away.

Think you these longing eyes,
        Though sick and spent,
And almost famish'd, ever will consent
        To leave those skies,
That glass of souls and spirits, where well drest
    They shine in white (like stars) and rest.

Shall my short hour, my inch,
        My one poor sand,
And crum of life, now ready to disband
        Revolt and flinch,
And having born the burthen all the day,
    Now cast at night my Crown away?

No, No; I am not he,
Go seek elsewhere.
I skill not your fine tinsel, and false hair,
Your Sorcery
And smooth seducements: I'le not stuff my story
With your Commonwealth and glory.

There are, that will sow tares
And scatter death
Amongst the quick, selling their souls and breath
For any wares;
But when thy Master comes, they'l finde and see
There's a reward for them and thee.

Then keep the antient way!
Spit out their phlegm
And fill thy brest with home; think on thy dream:
A calm, bright day!
A Land of flowers and spices! the word given,
If these be fair, O what is Heaven!

Cock-crowing

Father of lights! what Sunnie seed,
What glance of day hast thou confin'd
Into this bird? To all the breed
This busie Ray thou hast assign'd;
       Their magnetisme works all night,
       And dreams of Paradise and light.

Their eyes watch for the morning hue,
Their little grain expelling night
So shines and sings, as if it knew
The path unto the house of light.
       It seems their candle, howe'r done,
       Was tinn'd and lighted at the sunne.

If such a tincture, such a touch,
So firm a longing can impowre
Shall thy own image think it much
To watch for thy appearing hour?
       If a meer blast so fill the sail,
       Shall not the breath of God prevail?

O thou immortall light and heat!
Whose hand so shines through all this frame,
That by the beauty of the seat,
We plainly see, who made the same.
       Seeing thy seed abides in me,
       Dwell thou in it, and I in thee.

To sleep without thee, is to die;
Yea, 'tis a death partakes of hell:
For where thou dost not close the eye
It never opens, I can tell.
       In such a dark, Ægyptian border,
       The shades of death dwell and disorder.

If joyes, and hopes, and earnest throws,
And hearts, whose Pulse beats still for light
Are given to birds; who, but thee, knows
A love-sick souls exalted flight?
     Can souls be track'd by any eye
     But his, who gave them wings to flie?

Onely this Veyle which thou hast broke,
And must be broken yet in me,
This veyle, I say, is all the cloke
And cloud which shadows thee from me.
     This veyle thy full-ey'd love denies,
     And onely gleams and fractions spies.

O take it off! make no delay,
But brush me with thy light, that I
May shine unto a perfect day,
And warme me at thy glorious Eye!
     O take it off! or till it flee,
     Though with no Lilie, stay with me!

The Starre

What ever 'tis, whose beauty here below
Attracts thee thus & makes thee stream & flow,
    And wind and curle, and wink and smile,
        Shifting thy gate and guile:

Though thy close commerce nought at all imbarrs
My present search, for Eagles eye not starrs,
    And still the lesser by the best
        And highest good is blest:

Yet, seeing all things that subsist and be,
Have their Commissions from Divinitie,
    And teach us duty, I will see
        What man may learn from thee.

First, I am sure, the Subject so respected
Is well disposed, for bodies once infected,
    Deprav'd or dead, can have with thee
        No hold, nor sympathie.

Next, there's in it a restless, pure desire
And longing for thy bright and vitall fire,
    Desire that never will be quench'd,
        Nor can be writh'd, nor wrench'd.

These are the Magnets which so strongly move
And work all night upon thy light and love.
    As beauteous shapes, we know not why,
        Command and guide the eye.

For where desire, celestiall, pure desire
Hath taken root, and grows, and doth not tire,
    There God a Commerce states, and sheds
        His Secret on their heads.

This is the Heart he craves; and who so will
But give it him, and grudge not; he shall feel
That God is true, as herbs unseen
Put on their youth and green.

The Favour

O thy bright looks! thy glance of love
Shown, & but shown me from above!
Rare looks! that can dispense such joy
As without wooing wins the coy.
And makes him mourn, and pine and dye
Like a starv'd Eaglet, for thine eye.
Some kinde herbs here, though low & far,
Watch for, and know their loving star.
O let no star compare with thee!
Nor any herb out-duty me!
So shall my nights and mornings be
Thy time to shine, and mine to see.

The Bird

Hither thou com'st: the busie wind all night
Blew through thy lodging, where thy own warm wing
Thy pillow was. Many a sullen storm
(For which course man seems much the fitter born,)
      Rain'd on thy bed
      And harmless head.

And now as fresh and chearful as the light
Thy little heart in early hynms doth sing
Unto that *Providence*, whose unseen arm
Curb'd them, and cloath'd thee well and warm.
      All things that be, praise him; and had
      Their lesson taught them, when first made.

So hills and valleys into singing break,
And though poor stones have neither speech nor tongue,
While active winds and streams both run and speak,
Yet stones are deep in admiration.
Thus Praise and Prayer here beneath the Sun
Make lesser mornings, when the great are done.

For each inclosed Spirit is a star
      Inlightning his own little sphaere,
Whose light, though fetcht and borrowed from far,
      Both mornings makes, and evenings there.

But as these Birds of light make a land glad,
Chirping their solemn Matins on each tree:
So in the shades of night some dark fowls be,
Whose heavy notes make all that hear them, sad.

      The Turtle then in Palm-trees mourns,
          While Owls and Satyrs howl;
      The pleasant Land to brimstone turns
          And all her streams grow foul.

Brightness and mirth, and love and faith, all flye,
Till the Day-spring breaks forth again from high.

The Timber

Sure thou didst flourish once! and many Springs,
Many bright mornings, much dew, many showers
Past ore thy head: many light *Hearts* and *Wings*
Which now are dead, lodg'd in thy living bowers.

And still a new succession sings and flies;
Fresh Groves grow up, and their green branches shoot
Towards the old and still enduring skies,
While the low *Violet* thrives at their root.

But thou beneath the sad and heavy *Line*
Of death, dost waste all senseless, cold and dark;
Where not so much as dreams of light may shine,
Nor any thought of greenness, leaf or bark.

And yet (as if some deep hate and dissent,
Bred in thy growth betwixt high winds and thee,
Were still alive) thou dost great storms resent
Before they come, and know'st how near they be.

Else all at rest thou lyest, and the fierce breath
Of tempests can no more disturb thy ease;
But this thy strange resentment after death
Means onely those, who broke (in life) thy peace.

So murthered man, when lovely life is done,
And his blood freez'd, keeps in the Center still
Some secret sense, which makes the dead blood run
At his approach, that did the body kill.

And is there any murth'rer worse then sin?
Or any storms more foul then a lewd life?
Or what *Resentient* can work more within,
Then true remorse, when with past sins at strife?

He that hath left lifes vain joys and vain care,
And truly hates to be detain'd on earth,
Hath got an house where many mansions are,
And keeps his soul unto eternal mirth.

But though thus dead unto the world, and ceas'd
From sin, he walks a narrow, private way;
Yet grief and old wounds make him sore displeas'd,
And all his life a rainy, weeping day.

For though he should forsake the world, and live
As meer a stranger, as men long since dead;
Yet joy it self will make a right soul grieve
To think, he should be so long vainly lead.

But as shades set off light, so tears and grief
(Though of themselves but a sad blubber'd story)
By shewing the sin great, shew the relief
Far greater, and so speak my Saviors glory.

If my way lies through deserts and wilde woods;
Where all the Land with scorching heat is curst;
Better, the pools should flow with rain and floods
To fill my bottle, then I die with thirst.

Blest showers they are, and streams sent from above
Begetting *Virgins* where they use to flow;
And trees of life no other waters love,
These upper springs and none else make them grow.

But, these chaste fountains flow not till we dye;
Some drops may fall before, but a clear spring
And ever running, till we leave to fling
Dirt in her way, will keep above the skie.

Romans 6.7
He that is dead, is freed from sin.

Begging

I, do not go! thou know'st, I'le dye!
My *Spring* and *Fall* are in thy book!
Or, if thou goest, do not deny
To lend me, though from far, one look!

My sins long since have made thee strange,
A very stranger unto me;
No morning-meetings since this change,
Nor evening-walks have I with thee.

Why is my God thus slow and cold,
When I am most, most sick and sad?
Well fare those blessed days of old
When thou didst hear the *weeping Lad*!

O do not thou do as I did,
Do not despise a Love-sick heart!
What though some clouds defiance bid
Thy Sun must shine in every part.

Though I have spoil'd, O spoil not thou!
Hate not thine own dear gift and token!
Poor birds sing best, and prettiest show,
When their nest is faln and broken.

Dear Lord! restore thy ancient peace,
Thy quikning friendship, mans bright wealth!
And if thou wilt not give me ease
From sicknesse, give my spirit health!

The Seed growing secretly

Mark 4.26

If this worlds friends might see but once
What some poor man may often feel,
Glory, and gold, and Crowns and Thrones
They would soon quit and learn to kneel.

My dew, my dew! my early love,
My souls bright food, thy absence kills!
Hover not long, eternal Dove!
Life without thee is loose and spills.

Somthing I had, which long ago
Did learn to suck, and sip, and taste,
But now grown sickly, sad and slow,
Doth fret and wrangle, pine and waste.

O spred thy sacred wings and shake
One living drop! one drop life keeps!
If pious griefs Heavens joys awake,
O fill his bottle! thy childe weeps!

Slowly and sadly doth he grow,
And soon as left, shrinks back to ill;
O feed that life, which makes him blow
And spred and open to thy will!

For thy eternal, living wells
None stain'd or wither'd shall come near:
A fresh, immortal *green* there dwells,
And spotless *white* is all the wear.

Dear, secret *Greenness*! nurst below
Tempests and windes, and winter-nights,
Vex not, that but one sees thee grow,
That *One* made all these lesser lights.

If those bright joys he singly sheds
On thee, were all met in one Crown,
Both Sun and Stars would hide their heads;
And Moons, though full, would get them down.

Let glory be their bait, whose mindes
Are all too high for a low Cell:
Though Hawks can prey through storms and winds,
The poor Bee in her hive must dwel.

Glory, the Crouds cheap tinsel still
To what most takes them, is a drudge;
And they too oft take good for ill,
And thriving vice for vertue judge.

What needs a Conscience calm and bright
Within it self an outward test?
Who breaks his glass to take more light,
Makes way for storms into his rest.

Then bless thy secret growth, nor catch
At noise, but thrive unseen and dumb;
Keep clean, bear fruit, earn life and watch
Till the white winged Reapers come!

¶

As time one day by me did pass
   Through a large dusky glasse
   He held, I chanc'd to look
   And spyed his curious book
Of past days, where sad Heav'n did shed
A mourning light upon the dead.

Many disordered lives I saw
   And foul records which thaw
   My kinde eyes still, but in
   A fair, white page of thin
And ev'n, smooth lines, like the Suns rays,
Thy name was writ, and all thy days.

O bright and happy Kalendar!
   Where youth shines like a star
   All pearl'd with tears, and may
   Teach age, *The Holy way*;
Where through thick pangs, high agonies
Faith into life breaks, and death dies.

As some meek *night-piece* which day quails,
   To candle-light unveils:
   So by one beamy line
   From thy bright lamp did shine,
In the same page thy humble grave
Set with green herbs, glad hopes and brave.

Here slept my thoughts dear mark! which dust
   Seem'd to devour, like rust;
   But dust (I did observe)
   By hiding doth preserve,
As we for long and sure recruits,
Candy with sugar our choice fruits.

O calm and sacred bed where lies
    In deaths dark mysteries
    A beauty far more bright
    Then the noons cloudless light
For whose dry dust green branches bud
And robes are bleach'd in the *Lambs* blood.

Sleep happy ashes! (blessed sleep!)
    While haplesse I still weep;
    Weep that I have out-liv'd
    My life, and unreliev'd
Must (soul-lesse shadow!) so live on,
Though life be dead, and my joys gone.

¶

Fair and yong light! my guide to holy
Grief and soul-curing melancholy;
Whom living here I did still shun
As sullen night-ravens do the Sun,
And lead by my own foolish fire
Wandred through darkness, dens and mire.
How am I now in love with all
That I term'd then meer bonds and thrall,
And to thy name, which still I keep,
Like the surviving turtle, weep!
O bitter curs'd delights of men!
Our souls diseases first, and then
Our bodies; poysons that intreat
With fatal sweetness, till we eat;
How artfully do you destroy,
That kill with smiles and seeming joy?
If all the subtilties of vice
Stood bare before unpractic'd eyes,
And every act she doth commence
Had writ down its sad consequence,
Yet would not men grant, their ill fate
Lodged in those false looks, till too late.
O holy, happy, healthy heaven,
Where all is pure, where all is even,
Plain, harmless, faithful, fair and bright,
But what Earth breaths against thy light!
How blest had men been, had their *Sire*
Liv'd still in league with thy chaste fire,
Nor made life through her long descents,
A slave to lustful Elements!
I did once read in an old book
Soil'd with many a weeping look,
That the seeds of foul sorrows be
The finest things that are, to see.

So that fam'd fruit which made all dye
Seem'd fair unto the womans eye.
If these supplanters in the shade
Of Paradise, could make man fade,
How in this world should they deter
This world, their fellow-murtherer!
And why then grieve we to be sent
Home by our first fair punishment,
Without addition to our woes
And lingring wounds from weaker foes?
Since that doth quickly freedom win,
For he that's dead, is freed from sin.

O that I were winged and free
And quite undrest just now with thee,
Where freed souls dwel by living fountains
On everlasting, spicy mountains!
     Alas! my God! take home thy sheep;
     This world but laughs at those that weep.

Childe-hood

I cannot reach it; and my striving eye
Dazles at it, as at eternity.
    Were now that Chronicle alive,
Those white designs which children drive,
And the thoughts of each harmless hour,
With their content too in my pow'r,
Quickly would I make my path even,
And by meer playing go to Heaven.
    Why should men love
A Wolf more then a Lamb or Dove?
Or choose hell-fire and brimstone streams
Before bright stars, and Gods own beams?
Who kisseth thorns, will hurt his face,
But flowers do both refresh and grace,
And sweetly living (*fie on men!*)
Are when dead, medicinal then.
If seeing much should make staid eyes,
And long experience should make wise;
Since all that age doth teach, is ill,
Why should I not love childe-hood still?
Why if I see a rock or shelf,
Shall I from thence cast down my self,
Or by complying with the world,
From the same precipice be hurl'd?
Those observations are but foul
Which make me wise to lose my soul.

And yet the *Practice* worldlings call
Business and weighty action all,
Checking the poor childe for his play,
But gravely cast themselves away.

Dear, harmless age! the short, swift span,
Where weeping virtue parts with man;
Where love without lust dwells, and bends
What way we please, without self-ends.

An age of mysteries! which he
Must live twice, that would Gods face see;
Which *Angels* guard, and with it play,
Angels! which foul men drive away.

How do I study now, and scan
Thee, more then ere I studyed man,
And onely see through a long night
Thy edges, and thy bordering light!
O for thy Center and mid-day!
For sure that is the *narrow way*.

The Night

John 2.3

Through that pure *Virgin-shrine*,
That sacred vail drawn o'r thy glorious noon
That men might look and live as Glo-worms shine,
    And face the Moon:
    Wise *Nicodemus* saw such light
    As made him know his God by night.

    Most blest believer he!
Who in that land of darkness and blinde eyes
Thy long expected healing wings could see,
    When thou didst rise,
    And what can never more be done,
    Did at mid-night speak with the Sun!

    O who will tell me, where
He found thee at that dead and silent hour!
What hallow'd solitary ground did bear
    So rare a flower,
    Within whose sacred leafs did lie
    The fulness of the Deity.

    No mercy-seat of gold,
No dead and dusty *Cherub*, nor carv'd stone,
But his own living works did my Lord hold
    And lodge alone;
    Where *trees* and *herbs* did watch and peep
    And wonder, while the *Jews* did sleep.

    Dear night! this worlds defeat;
The stop to busie fools; cares check and curb;
The day of Spirits; my souls calm retreat
    Which none disturb!
    Christs progress, and his prayer time;
    The hours to which high Heaven doth chime.

Gods silent, searching flight:
When my Lords head is fill'd with dew, and all
His locks are wet with the clear drops of night;
          His still, soft call;
     His knocking time; The souls dumb watch,
     When Spirits their fair kinred catch.

          Were all my loud, evil days
Calm and unhaunted as is thy dark Tent,
Whose peace but by some *Angels* wing or voice
          Is seldom rent;
     Then I in Heaven all the long year
     Would keep, and never wander here.

          But living where the Sun
Doth all things wake, and where all mix and tyre
Themselves and others, I consent and run
          To ev'ry myre,
     And by this worlds ill-guiding light,
     Erre more then I can do by night.

          There is in God (some say)
A deep, but dazling darkness; As men here
Say it is late and dusky, because they
          See not all clear;
     O for that night! where I in him
     Might live invisible and dim.

Anguish

My God and King! to thee
I bow my knee,
I bow my troubled soul, and greet
With my foul heart thy holy feet.
Cast it, or tread it! It shall do
Even what thou wilt, and praise thee too.

My God, could I weep blood,
Gladly I would;
Or if thou wilt give me that Art,
Which through the eyes pours out the hart,
I will exhaust it all, and make
My self all tears, a weeping lake.

O! 'tis an easie thing
To write and sing;
But to write true, unfeigned verse
Is very hard! O God, disperse
These weights, and give my spirit leave
To act as well as to conceive!

O my God, hear my cry;
Or let me dye! ——

The Agreement

I wrote it down. But one that saw
And envyed that Record, did since
Such a mist over my minde draw,
It quite forgot that purpos'd glimpse.
　　I read it sadly oft, but still
　　Simply believ'd, 'twas not my Quill;

At length, my lifes kinde Angel came,
And with his bright and busie wing
Scatt'ring that cloud, shewd me the flame
Which strait, like Morning-stars did sing,
　　And shine, and point me to a place,
　　Which all the year sees the Suns face.

O beamy book! O my mid-day
Exterminating fears and night!
The mount, whose white Ascendents may
Be in conjunction with true light!
　　My thoughts, when towards thee they move,
　　Glitter and kindle with thy love.

Thou art the oyl and the wine-house:
Thine are the present healing leaves,
Blown from the tree of life to us
By his breath whom my dead heart heaves.
　　Each page of thine hath true life in't,
　　And Gods bright minde exprest in print.

Most modern books are blots on thee,
Their doctrine chaff and windy fits:
Darken'd along, as their scribes be,
With those foul storms, when they were writ;
　　While the mans zeal lays out and blends
　　Onely self-worship and self-ends.

Thou art the faithful, pearly rock,
The Hive of beamy, living lights,
Ever the same, whose diffus'd stock
Entire still, wears out blackest nights.
    Thy lines are rays, the true Sun sheds;
    Thy leaves are healing wings he spreads.

For until thou didst comfort me,
I had not one poor word to say:
Thick busie clouds did multiply,
And said, I was no childe of day;
    They said, my own hands did remove
    That candle given me from above.

O God! I know and do confess
My sins are great and still prevail,
Most heynous sins and numberless!
But thy *Compassions* cannot fail.
    If thy sure mercies can be broken,
    Then all is true, my foes have spoken.

But while time runs, and after it
Eternity, which never ends,
Quite through them both, still infinite
Thy Covenant by *Christ* extends;
    No sins of frailty, nor of youth
    Can foil his merits, and thy truth.

And this I hourly finde, for thou
Dost still renew, and purge and heal:
Thy care and love, which joyntly flow
New Cordials, new *Cathartics* deal.
    But were I once cast off by thee
    I know (my God!) this would not be.

Wherefore with tears (tears by thee sent)
I beg, my faith may never fail!
And when in death my speech is spent,

O let that silence then prevail!
    O chase in that *cold calm* my foes,
    And hear my hearts last private throws!

So thou, who didst the work begin
(For *I till drawn came not to thee*)
Wilt finish it, and by no sin
Will thy free mercies hindred be.
    For which, O God, I onely can
    Bless thee, and blame unthankful man.

The Water-fall

With what deep murmurs through times silent stealth
Doth thy transparent, cool and watry wealth
       Here flowing fall,
       And chide, and call,
As if his liquid, loose Retinue staid
Lingring, and were of this steep place afraid,
       The common pass
       Where, clear as glass,
       All must descend
       Not to an end:
But quickned by this deep and rocky grave,
Rise to a longer course more bright and brave.

      Dear stream! dear bank, where often I
      Have sate, and pleas'd my pensive eye,
      Why, since each drop of thy quick store
      Runs thither, whence it flow'd before,
      Should poor souls fear a shade or night,
      Who came (sure) from a sea of light?
      Or since those drops are all sent back
      So sure to thee, that none doth lack,
      Why should frail flesh doubt any more
      That what God takes, hee'l not restore?
      O useful Element and clear!
      My sacred wash and cleanser here,
      My first consigner unto those
      Fountains of life, where the Lamb goes?
      What sublime truths, and wholesome themes,
      Lodge in thy mystical, deep streams!
      Such as dull man can never finde
      Unless that Spirit lead his minde,
      Which first upon thy face did move,
      And hatch'd all with his quickning love.
      As this loud brooks incessant fall

In streaming rings restagnates all,
Which reach by course the bank, and then
Are no more seen, just so pass men.
O my invisible estate,
My glorious liberty, still late!
Thou art the Channel my soul seeks,
Not this with Cataracts and Creeks.

Quickness

False life! a foil and no more, when
            Wilt thou be gone?
Thou foul deception of all men
That would not have the true come on.

Thou art a Moon-like toil; a blinde
            Self-posing state;
A dark contest of waves and winde;
A meer tempestuous debate.

Life is a fix'd, discerning light,
            A knowing Joy;
No chance, or fit: but ever bright,
And calm and full, yet doth not cloy.

'Tis such a blissful thing, that still
            Doth vivifie,
And shine and smile, and hath the skill
To please without Eternity.

Thou art a toylsom Mole, or less
            A moving mist
But life is, what none can express,
A quickness, which my God hath kist.

The Quere

O tell me whence that joy doth spring
Whose diet is divine and fair,
Which wears heaven, like a bridal ring,
And tramples on doubts and despair?

Whose Eastern traffique deals in bright
And boundless Empyrean themes,
Mountains of spice, Day-stars and light,
Green trees of life, and living streams?

Tell me, O tell who did thee bring
And here, without my knowledge, plac'd,
Till thou didst grow and get a wing,
A wing with eyes, and eyes that taste?

Sure, *holyness* the *Magnet* is,
And *Love* the *Lure*, that woos thee down:
Which makes the high transcendent bliss
Of knowing thee, so rarely known.

The Book

Eternal God! maker of all
That have liv'd here, since the mans fall;
The Rock of ages! in whose shade
They live unseen, when here they fade.

Thou knew'st this *papyr*, when it was
Meer *seed*, and after that but *grass*;
Before 'twas *drest* or *spun*, and when
Made *linen*, who did *wear* it then:
What were their lifes, their thoughts & deeds
Whither good *corn*, or fruitless *weeds*.

   Thou knew'st this *Tree*, when a green *shade*
Cover'd it, since a *Cover* made,
And where it flourish'd, grew and spread,
As if it never should be dead.

   Thou knew'st this harmless *beast*, when he
Did live and feed by thy decree
On each green thing; then slept (well fed)
Cloath'd with this *skin*, which now lies spred
A *Covering* o're this aged book,
Which makes me wisely weep and look
On my own dust; meer dust it is,
But not so dry and clean as this.
Thou knew'st and saw'st them all and though
Now scatter'd thus, dost know them so.

   O knowing, glorious spirit! when
Thou shalt restore trees, beasts and men,
When thou shalt make all new again,
Destroying onely death and pain,
Give him amongst thy works a place,
Who in them lov'd and sought thy face!

To the Holy Bible

O book! lifes guide! how shall we part,
And thou so long seiz'd of my heart!
Take this last kiss, and let me weep
True thanks to thee, before I sleep.
   Thou wert the first put in my hand,
When yet I could not understand,
And daily didst my yong eyes lead
To letters, till I learnt to read.
But as rash youths, when once grown strong
Flye from their Nurses to the throng,
Where they new Consorts choose, & stick
To those, till either hurt or sick:
So with that first light gain'd from thee
Ran I in chase of vanity,
Cryed dross for gold, and never thought
My first cheap Book had all I sought.
Long reign'd this vogue; and thou cast by
With meek, dumb looks didst woo mine eye,
And oft left open would'st convey
A sudden and most searching ray
Into my soul, with whose quick touch
Refining still, I strugled much.
By this milde art of love at length
Thou overcam'st my sinful strength,
And having brought me home, didst there
Shew me that pearl I sought elsewhere.
Gladness, and peace, and hope, and love,
The secret favors of the Dove,
Her quickning kindness, smiles and kisses,
Exalted pleasures, crowning blisses,
Fruition, union, glory, life
Thou didst lead to, and still all strife.
Living, thou wert my souls sure ease,
And dying mak'st me go in peace:

Thy next *Effects* no tongue can tell;
Farewel O book of God! farewel!

Luke 2.14

Glory be to God in the highest, and on
Earth peace, good will towards men.

From *Thalia Rediviva*

Looking Back

Fair, shining *Mountains* of my pilgrimage,
    And flow'ry *Vales*, whose flow'rs were stars:
The *days* and *nights* of my first, happy age;
    An age without distast and warrs:
When I by thoughts ascend your *Sunny heads*,
    And mind those sacred, *midnight* Lights:
By which I walk'd, when curtain'd Rooms and Beds
    Confin'd, or seal'd up others sights:
        O then how bright
        And quick a light
    Doth brush my heart and scatter night;
        Chasing that shade
        Which my sins made,
While I so *spring*, as if I could not *fade*!

How brave a prospect is a bright *Back-side*!
    Where flow'rs and palms refresh the Eye:
And days well spent like the glad *East* abide,
    Whose morning-glories cannot dye!

Retirement

Fresh *fields* and *woods*! the Earth's fair *face*,
God's *foot-stool*, and mans *dwelling-place*.
I ask not why the first *Believer*
Did love to be a Country liver?
Who to secure pious content
Did pitch by *groves* and *wells* his tent;
Where he might view the boundless *skie*,
And all those glorious *lights* on high:
With flying *meteors*, *mists* and *show'rs*,
Subjected *hills*, *trees*, *meads* and *Flow'rs*:
And ev'ry minute bless the King
And wise Creatour of each thing.
    I ask not why he did remove
To happy *Mamre's* holy grove,
Leaving the *Citie's* of the plain
To *Lot* and his successless train?
All various Lusts in *Cities* still
Are found; they are the *Thrones* of Ill.
The dismal *Sinks*, where blood is spill'd,
Cages with much uncleanness fill'd.
But *rural shades* are the sweet fense
Of piety and innocence.
They are the *Meek's* calm region, where
Angels descend, and rule the sphere:
Where heav'n lyes *Leiguer*, and the *Dove*
Duely as *Dew*, comes from above.
If *Eden* be on Earth at all,
'Tis that, which we the *Country* call.

The Bee

From fruitful *beds* and flowry *borders*
Parcell'd to wastful Ranks and Orders,
Where *state* grasps more than plain *Truth* needs
And wholesome *Herbs* are starv'd by *Weeds*:
To the wild Woods I will be gone,
And the course Meals of great *Saint John.*
     When truth and piety are mist
Both in the Rulers and the Priest;
When pity is not cold, but dead,
And the rich eat the Poor like bread;
While factious heads with open Coile
And force first make, then share the spoile:
To *Horeb* then *Elias* goes,
And in the *Desart* grows the *Rose.*
          Hail Christal Fountains and fresh shades,
                    Where no proud look invades.
No busie worldling hunts away
The sad Retirer all the day:
Haile happy harmless solitude,
Our Sanctuary from the rude
And scornful world: the calm recess
Of faith, and hope and holiness!
Here something still like *Eden* looks,
Hony in Woods, *Julips* in Brooks:
And *Flow'rs*, whose rich, unrifled *Sweets*
With a chast kiss the cool dew greets.
When the toyls of the Day are done
And the tir'd world sets with the Sun,
Here *flying* winds and *flowing* Wells
Are the wise, watchful Hermits *Bells*;
Their buisie *murmurs* all the night
To *praise* or *prayer* do invite,
And with an awful sound arrest

And piously employ his breast.
  When in the *East* the Dawn both blush,
Here cool, fresh *Spirits* the air brush;
Herbs (strait) get up, *Flow'rs* peep and spread:
Trees whisper praise, and bow the head.
Birds from the shades of night release
Look round about, then quit the neast,
And with united gladness sing
The glory of the morning's King.
The *Hermit* hears, and with meek voice
Offers his own up, and their Joys:
Then prays, that all the world may be
Blest with as sweet an unity.
  If sudden storms the day invade,
They flock about him to the shade:
Where wisely they expect the end,
Giving the tempest time to spend;
And hard by shelters on some bough
Hilarion's servant, the sage *Crow*.
  O purer years of light, and grace!
The *diff'rence* is great, as the *space*
'Twixt you and us: who blindly run
After *false-fires*, and leave the *Sun*.
Is not fair *Nature* of her self
Much richer than dull *paint*, or *pelf?*
And are not *streams* at the *Spring-head*
More sweet than in carv'd *Stone*, or *Lead?*
But *fancy* and some *Artist's* tools
Frame a Religion for fools.
  The *truth*, which once was plainly taught,
With *thorns* and *briars* now is fraught.
Some part is with bold *Fables* spotted,
Some by strange *Comments* wildly blotted:
And *discord* (old Corruption's Crest,)
With *blood* and *blame* hath stain'd the rest.

So *Snow*, which in its first descents
A whiteness, like pure heav'n presents,
When touch'd by *Man* is quickly soil'd
And after trodden down, and spoil'd.
      O lead me, where I may be free
In *truth* and *Spirit* to serve thee!
Where undisturb'd I may converse
With thy great self, and there rehearse
Thy gifts with thanks, and from thy store
Who art all blessings, beg much more!
Give me the Wisdom of the *Bee*,
And her unwearied Industry:
That from the *wild Gourds* of these days
I may extract Health and thy praise;
Who can'st turn darkness into light,
And in my weakness shew thy might!
      Suffer me not in any want
To seek refreshment from a *Plant*,
Thou did'st not *set*! since all must be
Pluck'd up, whose *growth* is not from thee.
'Tis not the *garden* and the *Bowrs*,
Nor *fense* and *forms* that give to flow'rs
Their *wholsomness*: but thy *good will*,
Which *truth* and *pureness* purchase still.
      Then since corrupt man hath driv'n hence
Thy kind and saving *Influence*,
And *Balm* is no more to be had
In all the Coasts of *Gilead*:
Go with me to the *shade* and *cell*,
Where thy best *Servants* once did dwell.
There let me know thy *Will*, and see
Exil'd *Religion* own'd by thee.
For thou can'st turn dark *Grots* to *Halls*,
And make *Hills* blossome like the *vales*:
Decking their untill'd *heads* with flow'rs

And fresh delights for all sad hours:
Till from them, like a laden *Bee*,
I may fly home, and *hive* with thee.

DAPHNIS
An Elegiac *Eclogue*

The Interlocutors: *Damon, Menalcas*

Da. What clouds, *Menalcas*, do oppress thy brow?
Flow'rs in a Sunshine never look so low.
Is *Nisa* still cold Flint? or have thy Lambs
Met with the Fox by straying from their Dams?

Men. Ah! *Damon*, no; my Lambs are safe, & she
Is kind, and much more white than they can be.
But what doth life, when most serene, afford
Without a worm, which gnaws her fairest gourd?
Our days of gladness are but short reliefs,
Giv'n to reserve us for enduring griefs.
So smiling Calms close Tempests breed, wch break
Like spoilers out, and kill our flocks, when weak.
    I heard last *May* (and *May* is still high Spring,)
The pleasant *Philomel* her Vespers sing.
The green wood glitter'd with the golden Sun
And all the West like Silver shin'd; not one
Black cloud, no rags, nor spots did stain
The Welkins beauty: nothing frown'd like rain;
But e're night came, that Scene of fine sights turn'd
To fierce dark showrs; the Air with lightnings burn'd;
The woods sweet Syren rudely thus opprest,
Gave to the Storm her weak and weary Breast.
I saw her next day on her last cold bed;
And *Daphnis* so, just so is *Daphnis* dead!

Da. So Violets, so doth the Primrose fall,
At once the Springs pride and its funeral.
Such easy sweets get off still in their prime,
And stay not here, to wear the soil of Time.
While courser Flow'rs (which none would miss, if past;)
To scorching Summers, and cold Autumns last.

Men. Souls need not time, the early forward things
Are always fledg'd, and gladly use their Wings,
Or else great parts, when injur'd quit the Crowd,
To shine above still, not behind the Cloud.
And is't not just to leave those to the night,
That madly hate, and persecute the light?
Who doubly dark, all *Negroes* do exceed,
And inwardly are true black Moores indeed.

Da. The punishment still manifests the Sin,
As outward signs shew the disease within.
While worth opprest mounts to a nobler height,
And Palm-like bravely overtops the weight.
So where swift *Isca* from our lofty hills
With lowd farewels descends, and foming fills
A wider Channel, like some great port-vein,
With large rich streams to feed the humble plain:
I saw an Oak, whose stately height and shade
Projected far, a goodly shelter made,
And from the top with thick diffused Boughs
In distant rounds grew, like a Wood-nymphs house.
Here many Garlands won at Roundel-lays
Old shepheards hung up in those happy days,
With knots and girdles, the dear spoils and dress
Of such bright maids, as did true lovers bless.
And many times had old *Amphion* made
His beauteous Flock acquainted with this shade;
A Flock, whose fleeces were as smooth and white
As those, the wellkin shews in Moonshine night.
Here, when the careless world did sleep, have I
In dark records and numbers noblie high
The visions of our black, but brightest Bard
From old *Amphion*'s mouth full often heard;
With all those plagues poor shepheards since have known,
And Ridles more, which future times must own.
While on his pipe young *Hylas* plaid, and made

Musick as solemn as the song and shade.
But the curs'd owner from the trembling top
To the firm brink, did all those branches lop,
And in one hour what many years had bred,
The pride and beauty of the plain lay dead.
The undone Swains in sad songs mourn'd their loss,
While storms & cold winds did improve the Cross.
But Nature, which (like vertue) scorns to yield
Brought new recruits and succours to the Field;
For by next Spring the check'd Sap wak'd from sleep
And upwards still to feel the Sun did creep,
Till at those wounds, the hated Hewer made,
There sprang a thicker and a fresher shade.

   Men. So thrives afflicated Truth! and so the light,
When put out, gains a value from the Night.
How glad are we, when but one twinkling Star
Peeps betwixt clouds, more black than is our Tar?
And Providence was kind, that order'd this
To the brave Suff'rer should be solid bliss;
Nor is it so till this short life be done,
But goes hence with him, and is still his Sun.

   Da. Come Shepherds then, and with your greenest Bays
Refresh his dust, who lov'd your learned Lays.
Bring here the florid glories of the Spring,
And as you strew them pious *Anthems* sing,
Which to your children and the years to come
May speak of *Daphnis*, and be never dumb.
While prostrate I drop on his quiet Urn
My Tears, not gifts; and like the poor, that mourn
With green, but humble Turfs ; write o're his Hearse
For false, foul Prose-men this fair Truth in Verse.
   'Here *Daphnis* sleeps! & while the great watch goes
Of loud and restless Time, takes his repose.
Fame is but noise, all Learning but a thought:
Which one admires, another sets at nought.

Nature mocks both, and Wit still keeps adoe;
But Death brings knowledge and assurance too.'

Men. Cast in your Garlands, strew on all the flow'rs
Which *May* with smiles, or *April* feeds with show'rs.
Let this days Rites as stedfast as the Sun
Keep pace with Time, and through all Ages run,
The publick character and famous Test
Of our long sorrows and his lasting rest;
And when we make procession on the plains,
Or yearly keep the Holyday of Swains,
Let *Daphnis* still be the recorded name
And solemn honour of our feasts and fame.
For though the *Isis* and the prouder *Thames*
Can shew his reliques lodg'd hard by their streams.
And must for ever to the honour'd name
Of Noble *Murrey* chiefly owe that fame:
Yet, here his Stars first saw him, and when fate
Beckon'd him hence, it knew no other date.
Nor will these vocal Woods and Valleys fail,
Nor *Isca's* lowder Streams this to bewail,
But while Swains hope and Seasons change, will glide
With moving murmurs, because *Daphnis* di'd.

Da. A fatal sadness, such as still foregoes,
Then runs along with publick plagues and woes,
Lies heavy on us, and the very light
Turn'd Mourner too, hath the dull looks of Night.
Our vales like those of Death, a darkness shew
More sad than Cypress, or the gloomy Yew,
And on our hills, where health with height complied,
Thick drowsie Mists hang round and there reside.
Not one short parcel of the tedious year
In its old dress and beauty doth appear;
Flowr's hate the Spring, and with a sullen bend
Thrust down their Heads, which to the Root still tend,
And thought the Sun like a cold Lover, peeps

A little at them, still the Days-eye sleeps.
But when the Crab and Lion with acute
And active Fires their sluggish heat recruit,
Our grass straight russets, and each scorching day
Drinks up our Brooks as fast as dew in May.
Till the sad Heardsman with his Cattel faints,
And empty Channels ring with loud Complaints.

   Men. Heaven's just displeasure & our unjust ways
Change Natures course, bring plagues dearth and decays.
This turns our lands to Dust, the skies to Brass,
Makes old kind blessings into curses pass.
And when we learn unknown and forraign Crimes,
Brings in the vengeance due unto those Climes.
The dregs and puddle of all ages now
Like Rivers near their fall, on us do flow.
Ah happy *Daphnis!* who, while yet the streams
Ran clear & warm (though but with setting beams,)
Got through: and saw by that declining light
His toil's and journey's end before the Night.

   Da. A night, where darkness lays her chains and Bars.
And feral fires appear instead of Stars
But he along with the last looks of day
Went hence, and setting (Sun-like) past away.
What future storms our present sins do hatch
Some in the dark discern, and others watch;
Though foresight makes no Hurricane prove mild;
Fury that's long fermenting, is most wild.
   But see, while thus our sorrows we discourse,
Phoebus hath finish't his diurnal course.
The shades prevail, each Bush seems bigger grown:
Darkness (like State,) makes small things swell and frown.
The Hills and Woods with Pipes and Sonnets round
And bleating sheep our Swains drive home, resound.

Men. What voice from yonder Lawn tends hither? heark
'Tis *Thyrsis* calls, I hear *Lycanthe* bark.
His Flocks left out so late, and weary grown
Are to the Thickets gone, and there laid down.

Da. Menalcas, haste to look them out, poor sheep
When day is done, go willingly to sleep.
And could bad Man his time spend, as they do,
He might go sleep, or die, as willing too.

Men. Farewel kind *Damon*! now the Shepheards Star
With beauteous looks smiles on us, though from far.
All creatures that were favourites of day
Are with the Sun retir'd and gone away.
While feral Birds send forth unpleasant notes,
And night (the Nurse of thoughts,) sad thoughts promotes.
But Joy will yet come with the morning-light,
Though sadly now we bid good night! *Da.* good night!

Letter to his cousin, Aubrey

To Aubrey

Honoured Cousin.

I received yours & should have gladly served you, had it bine in my power. butt all my search & consultations with those few that I could suspect to have any knowledge of Antiquitie, came to nothing; for the antient Bards (though by the testimonie of their Enemies, the Romans;) a very learned societie: yet (like the Druids) they communicated nothing of their knowledge, butt by way of tradition: wch I suppose to be the reason that we have no account left vs: nor any sort of remains, or other monuments of their learning, or way of living.

As to the later Bards, who were no such men, butt had a societie & some rules & orders among themselves: & several sorts of measures & a kind of Lyric poetrie: wch are all sett down exactly In the learned John David Rhees, or Rhesus his welch, or British grammer: you shall have there (in the later end of his book) a most curious Account of them. This vein of poetrie they called Awen, which in their language signifies as much as Raptus, or a poetic furor; & (in truth) as many of them as I have conversed with are (as I may say) gifted or inspired with it. I was told by a very sober & knowing person (now dead) that in his time, there was a young lad father & motherless, & soe very poor that he was forced to beg; butt att last was taken vp by a rich man, that kept a great stock of sheep vpon the mountains not far from the place where I now dwell. who cloathed him & sent him into the mountains to keep his sheep. There in Summer time following the sheep & looking to their lambs, he fell into a deep sleep; In wch he dreamt, that he saw a beautifull young man with a garland of green leafs vpon his head, & an hawk vpon his fist: with a quiver full of Arrows att his back, coming towards him (whistling several measures or tunes all the way) & att last lett the hawk fly att him, w^ch (he dreamt) gott into his mouth & inward parts, & suddenly awaked in a great fear & consternation: butt possessed with such a vein, or gift of poetrie, that he left the sheep & went about the Countrey, making songs vpon all occasions, and came to be the most famous Bard in all the Countrey in his time.

Dear Cousin I should & would be very ready to serve you in any thing wherein I may be usefull, or qualified to doe it, & I give you my heartie thanks for yor continued affections & kind remembrances of

S^r

Yo^r most obliged & faithfull

Servant,

Hen: Vaughan

Select Bibliography

Stevie Davies, *Henry Vaughan*, Seren Books, 1995.

L. C. Martin, *Henry Vaughan: Poetry and Selected Prose*, second edition, Oxford University Press, 1963.

Jonathan F. S. Post, *Henry Vaughan, The Unfolding Vision*, Princeton University Press, 1992.

Alan Rudrum, *Henry Vaughan* (Writers of Wales series), University of Wales Press, 1981.

Alan Rudrum, ed., *Essential Articles for the Study of Henry Vaughan*, Archon Books, 1987.

Alan Rudrum, ed., *Henry Vaughan, The Complete Poems*, Penguin Classics, 1976.

Evelyn Underhill, *Mysticism,* Oneworld Publications, 1993.

Scintilla, yearly journal of the Usk Valley Vaughan Association (since 1997).

Index of Poems

Lightning Source UK Ltd.
Milton Keynes UK
UKHW021346120522
402894UK00005B/236

9 780281 055425